PROGRESS IN UNITY?

LOUVAIN THEOLOGICAL & PASTORAL MONOGRAPHS
18

PROGRESS IN UNITY?

FIFTY YEARS OF THEOLOGY WITHIN THE WORLD COUNCIL OF CHURCHES: 1945-1995 A STUDY GUIDE

by Martien E. Brinkman

PEETERS PRESS
LOUVAIN

W.B. EERDMANS

Cover: Cryptogram on the tomb of Antonia in the catacombs of Domitilla in
Rome: one of the earliest signs of Christian unity.

ISBN 90-6831-684-2
D. 1995/0602/33

TABLE OF CONTENTS

FOREWORD

This study guide does not deal with the history of the ecumenical movement, nor does it deal with the history of the World Council of Churches Commission on Faith and Order. It deals with an assessment of the scope of the ecumenical agreement which has been reached around a great many central themes within world Christianity during the past fifty years. Within the World Council of Churches, Faith and Order is more or less the point of crystallization of this agreement, which is the reason why this study is also rather strongly focused on the work of this commission.

The principal motive for publication of this study lies in the supposition that the official institutional ecumenical movement has added a unique dimension to the Christian discussion of faith. This unique dimension is especially to be found in the fruitful interaction brought about by the ecumenical movement between the various church traditions and between the various continents. Thereby a dynamic process of transmission of faith traditions has been set going, as a result of which the realization is gaining ground that the diverse Christian traditions relate to one another in in a complementary fashion. That is the reason why there has been a growing realization that the various traditions need each other in order to be safeguarded from forms of onesidedness and in order to preserve the orientation towards the full range of the prophetic and apostolic proclamation.

With a view to elaborating this supposition, attention will particularly be focused on the *results* of the world-wide discussion of faith and not so much on the sometimes long and laborious genesis of these results. With regard to the latter, one may always consult the studies mentioned in the bibliography. Of course, it will also be continually necessary to describe brief historical positions in broad outline. On these occasions, however, a short introduction and further reference will, as a rule, suffice.

In my opinion, the great ecumenical shortcoming now lies not so much in an insufficiently profound analysis of the history of the doctrinal differences between the various Christian traditions, but rather in a too limited reception of the ecumenical agreement which has already been reached on the basis of the content of the numerous historical studies. Hence, this study guide takes as its point of departure, in particular, those ecumenical publications which summarize the *results* of the ecumenical reflection of the past fifty years as succinctly as possible.

This concentration on the results of ecumenical reflection is prompted by more than the fact that, so far, these results are little known and, therefore, have been insufficiently integrated into systematic, liturgical or practical-theological reflection. Even there where a knowledge of the results of ecumenical dialogues is present, these results have not always been existentially digested, so to speak, and are therefore not evident in either personal or ecclesial stands on issues. There is no doubt that the sometimes strictly separated circuits – the academic, systematic-theological circuit on the one hand, and the ecclesial, ecumenical circuit on the other hand – play a part in this, but another reason is a certain kind of ecumenical laziness, as a result of which the ecumenically achieved result is often looked upon as a finishing point instead of only as a beginning.

It is true that, on the publication of the so-called Lima text on Baptism, Eucharist and Ministry (BEM) a reception process of many years was consciously planned, but the reactions to this text on the part of the member churches make it patently clear that it is not easy to organize such a process world-wide. There have been few reactions from the relatively young churches of the southern hemisphere, and among the older churches of the northern hemisphere the response sometimes has not risen above the level of officials[1].

---

[1] See for the reactions of the churches, M. Thurian (ed.), *Churches Respond to BEM*, Vol.I-VI (Faith and Order Papers Nos. 129;132; 135; 137; 143 and 144), Geneva 1986-1988 and the evaluation report, *Baptism, Eucharist & Ministry 1982-1990: Report on the Process and Responses* (Faith and Order Paper No. 149), Geneva 1990. See for the Lima text itself *Baptism, Eucharist and Ministry (Faith and Order Paper No. 111)*, Geneva 1982.

It is considerably easier to remedy the first impeding factor – the separated circuits, than the second – the scanty existential digestion. From the history and the present state of the ecumenical movement a lot of examples may be given of a strong commitment on the part of leading academic theologians in the field of, for example, exegesis, church history, liturgical studies, systematic theology and religious studies. And, conversely, a great many of those who are ecclesial-ecumenically committed are respected scholars, or have become so in time, partly as a result of their ecumenical publications. In academic circles, therefore, ignorance of the results of the ecumenical reflection may be rightly qualified as unscholarly. Meanwhile, in spite of the semblance of closed circuits, there are so many examples of a clearly visible and fruitful interaction (cross-fertilization) between the university and the 'church' as ecumenical movement that, for an exegete, historian, or dogmatician to be ignorant of the results of this interaction and exchange would testify to ignorance of his or her specialist literature.

The relations are far more complicated when it is a matter of the existential digestion of the results of ecumenical reflection. Such a processing always depends on a great many rather intangible factors. Even in a strategically planned 'reception process', of the sort that was embarked upon concerning the ecumenical convergence with respect to baptism, eucharist and ministry, such a process is in fact impossible to organize. However, it certainly is possible to create conditions for it and one of these conditions is the process of becoming acquainted, as best, one can, with the results of the ecumenical reflection and by a careful assessment of their content. In itself that is a sheer academic activity – as a result of which it ought to take place at the theological faculties. Apart from that, however, it is also an activity with considerable ecclesial consequences, namely, the growing recognition and acknowledgment of each other as Christians belonging to different traditions and different continents.

After a short introduction to the work of the World Council of Churches Commission on Faith and Order in general, a concise description of the remarkable ecumenical consensus between the Eastern Orthodox Churches and the Oriental Orthodox Churches in the field of christology, and between the churches of the East and the West in the field of pneumatology, will be offered. In the subsequent chapters, attention will be paid to the ecumenical rapprochement in the sense of convergence with respect to themes like Scripture and tradition, the common expression of our faith, baptism, eucharist and ministry.

The relationship between these, at first sight perhaps strongly ecclesio-centric, themes and the great issues of justice, peace and integrity of creation, which will continually be brought up for discussion in the various chapters, will be subject of more explicit discussion in the penultimate chapter under the heading of "Church and Kingdom". In the final chapter, the relation Ecumenicals-Evangelicals will be dealt with. In this way, the ecclesiological reflection is deliberately put against the background of the ellipse of, on the one hand, the perspective of the whole of God's world (oikoumene) and, on the other hand, the perspective of the specifically individual existential digestion of faith. It is only within this dual perspective of the faithful individual and salvation for the whole world that the ecclesiological issues of sacrament and ministry acquire their most profound significance.

The specific character of this study lies mainly in its summarizing character, in which we have attempted to follow as closely as possible the literal text of conference and council declarations. This appears not only from the many literal quotations, but also from the linking texts in which, in spite of the usual paraphrasing, an attempt is nevertheless made to follow as closely as possible the original language of the various documents.

As a point of departure for judging the results of the ecumenical discussion during the past fifty years, the principle has not always been applied that it is the most recent and the most authoritative documents – which, in the World Council of Churches, means: accepted by a World Assembly – which necessarily articulate the theme concerned most adequately. For that reason, older documents have sometimes deliberately been drawn upon. The fact that here, therefore, the author proffers a judgment will not, it is hoped, be regarded as a disadvantage, but rather as an advantage. Indeed, it is this which lends the character of challenge to our summarizing study.

In spite of these unmistakable, specific accents, the significance of this book is nevertheless mainly to be found in its evaluative character. It may become clear from this how refreshing and encouraging it may still be to get thoroughly acquainted with the results of those discussions of faith carried on for decades throughout the world. Lest we forget what, in spite of all discord, has been said by many church leaders and theologians in total frankness (parresia, cf. Acts. 4:13,29 and 31) and in public witness!

May this study guide, therefore, not only contribute to the *knowledge* of the results of almost fifty years of institutional ecumenical reflection within the World Council of Churches, but also to a dynamic lifeprocess of real sharing of those resources, in the light of which other fellow believers in other churches and other continents lead their concrete lives.

The text of this book was initially presented as lecture material at the Faculty of Theology of the Catholic University at Louvain (Belgium) under the auspices of the Hadrian VI Chair for Ecumenism. The opening lecture on 25 January 1994 concluded with the following phrase which I have tried to bear in mind continually, not only while delivering the lectures, but also while elaborating them in writing:

> *"It is a well-known fact that the great citizen of Utrecht who came to Louvain in 1476 afterwards as Pope Hadrian VI took a clear position of rejection with respect to Luther, without, meanwhile, being blind to the serious shortcomings which Luther pointed out in his church. As far as that was concerned, the instruction which he gave to his delegate Chierigati to the 'Reichstag' at Neurenberg in 1523 was certainly as plain as day.*
>
> *My prayer would be for my contribution to the exchange among the various Christians traditions, which the discipline of ecumenism has for its aim, to take place in a way which may follow the example of the way in which Hadrian VI was loyal and critical of himself with respect to his church, the Mother of all of us"* [2].

---

[2] Cf. for the text of the inaugural lecture M.E. Brinkman, "The Will to Common Confession: The Contribution of Calvinist Protestantism to the World Council of

As a Dutch Reformed theologian I am very pleased to be allowed to give this course of lectures at the Louvain faculty which has become so well-known through the Counter-Reformation. However paradoxical it may sound, it was precisely through the persecution of Reformed Protestantism in Belgium – the first Protestant martyrs, Hendrik Voes and Johannes van Esschen, died at the stake of the Great Market at Brussels in 1523 after Louvain theologians had established their heresy! – that Belgian Calvinist refugees had an enormous influence on Dutch Calvinism. We owe the *Confessio Belgica* (1561), called the *Nederlandse Geloofsbelijdenis* in the Netherlands, to Guido de Brès from Bray, in the neighborhood of Bergen (Mons); we owe the rhymed version of the psalms to Petrus Datheen from Berg(Mons)-Cassel and we are indebted to Marnix van Sint Aldegonde from Brussels for the so religiously charged Dutch national anthem[3]. Thus, historically shaped by what Belgians brought to the Netherlands, I now hope in a totally different historical setting, by way of the world-wide ecumenical dialogues organized by the World Council of Churches, to contribute my share to the mutual recognition of what has grown apart during almost five centuries.

Utrecht, January 1995

Churches Study Project 'Confessing the One Faith'", *Louvain Studies* 19 (1994) 118-137. See on the significance of Hadrian VI, for example, J.N.D. Kelly, *The Oxford Dictionary of Popes*, Oxford-New York 1986, 258-259.
[3] Cf. E. Pichal, *De geschiedenis van het protestantisme in Vlaanderen*, Antwerpen-Amsterdam 1975.

CHAPTER I

FAITH AND ORDER

A Short History of Faith and Order

Together with the movement for Life and Work and the International Missionary Council, the Faith and Order movement was a major expression of ecumenism during the first half of this century[1]. Following the 1910 World Missionary Conference in Edinburgh (Scotland), the convention of the (Anglican) Protestant Episcopal Church in the USA in 1910 called on church leaders from all over the world to convene a theological conference for the considering of questions touching 'faith' and 'order'. The Convention decided to appoint a Joint Commission to arrange for a World Conference of "all Christian Communions thoughout the world which confess our Lord Jesus Christ as God and Saviour". This work is to be undertaken in "the belief that the beginnings of unity are to be found in the clear statement and full consideration of those things in which we differ, as well as of those things in which we are at one"[2]. In its preparatory report the Commission deliberately speaks of questions of 'faith' and 'order':

---

[1] For a historical survey see G. Thils, *Histoire doctrinale du mouvement oecuménique*, Paris-Louvain 1962; J. Skoglund/J.R. Nelson, *Fifty Years of Faith and Order*, New York 1963; R. Frieling, *Die Bewegung für Glauben und Kirchenverfassung 1910-1937*, Göttingen 1970 and K.C. Epting, *Ein Gespräch beginnt: Die Anfänge der Bewegung für Glauben und Kirchenverfassung in den Jahren 1910-1920*, Zürich 1972.

[2] Cf. L. Vischer (ed.), *A Documentary History of the Faith & Order Movement 1927-1963*, St-Louis 1963, 199-201 ("Joint Commission Appointed to Arrange for a World Conference on Faith and Order. Report on Plan and Scope (1911)").

*"Of **Faith**, not of opinion, but of what is required or imposed as de fide, concerning God and Christ, concerning man and the future world; of **Order**, not of preferential practice, but of matters of discipline with regard to the Ministry, the Sacraments, Marriage and Christian Life"* [3].

After a preparatory meeting at Geneva (Switzerland) in 1920 the First World Conference on Faith and Order took place in Lausanne (Switzerland) in 1927[4]. It provided – so Günther Gassmann states in the 'Introduction' to his *Documentary History of Faith and Order*[5] – the first occasion in modern church history for over 400 participants from Orthodox, Anglican, Reformation and Free churches – together, representatives of 127 churches – to come together to discuss their agreements in faith and the deep differences which had divided them for centuries[6]. From these early years onwards, Faith and Order has viewed its theological task as

[3] Cf. *The World Conference for the Consideration of Questions touching Faith and Order: Report of the Joint Commission to the General Convention of the Protestant Episcopal Church 1916*, Gardiner 1916, 10. Cf. also with regard to the terminology of 'faith' and 'order', G. Gassmann, *Konzeptionen der Einheit in der Bewegung für Glauben und Kirchenverfassung 1910-1937*, Göttingen 1979, 49/50. See further the "Introduction" in L. Vischer (ed), *A Documentary History*, 7-23, esp. 8/9.
[4] Cf. H.N. Bate, *Faith and Order: Proceedings of the Word Conference Lausanne, August 3-21,1927*, Garden City 1928[2], esp. vii-xv ("Faith and Order,1910-1927"). See further T. Tatlow, "The World Conference on Faith and Order" in: R. Rouse/S.C. Neill (eds.), *A History of the Ecumenical Movement 1517-1948*, London 1954, 405-441.
[5] G. Gassmann, *Documentary History of Faith and Order 1963-1993* (Faith and Order Paper No. 159), Geneva 1993, 6-9. See also Idem, "Faith and Order" in: N. Lossky et al. (eds.), *Dictionary of the Ecumenical Movement*, Geneva-Grand Rapids 1991, 411-413. With a view to simplifying the traceability of the quotations from texts of the World Council of Churches, quotations will preferably be taken from the collections of documents by Gassmann. The original references are mentioned in his work and have sometimes also been mentioned in this study guide, when the text quoted cannot be found fully printed in Gassmann's anthology.
[6] Cf. the "Preamble" of the Final Report: "This is a Conference summoned to consider matters of Faith and Order. It is emphatically *not* attempting to define the conditions of future reunion. Its object is to register the apparent level of fundamental agreements within the Conference and the grave points of disagreements remaining; also to suggest certain lines of thought which may in the future tend to a fuller measure of agreement". See for the whole text of the Final Report, L. Vischer (ed.), *A Documentary History*, 27-39, esp. 27.

one of overcoming church-dividing differences and preparing the way towards visible unity.

The Second World Conference on Faith and Order in Edinburgh, in 1937, was more systematically prepared by a number of commissions. It followed the comparative methodology of registering agreements and disagreements, but was yet able to clarify several concepts of church unity, with a certain preference for that of organic or corporate union[7]. The conference also agreed to the proposal to unite the Faith and Order and Life and Work movements to form a council of churches. This decision was implemented at Amsterdam (The Netherlands) in 1948 when the World Council of Churches was founded.

Within the World Council of Churches the tasks of the Faith and Order movement were carried on by the Commission on Faith and Order. But the idea of a movement was preserved and expressed in the form of a special constitution which, for example, provides for membership in the Commission, of representatives from churches which do not exclusively belong to the World Council of Churches, and which creates the possibility for the Commission to continue to organize world conferences from time to time (Lausanne 1927, Edinburgh 1937, Lund 1952, Montreal 1963 and Santiago de Compostela 1993). The commission has a standing commission of 30 members. The whole commission of 120 representatives meets every three or four years. The aim of the Commission is

> "to proclaim the oneness of the church of Jesus Christ and to call the churches to the goal of visible unity in one faith and one eucharistic fellowship, expressed in worship and in common life in Christ, in order that the world may believe" (cf. John 17,21)[8].

---

[7] Cf. G. Gassmann, *Konzeptionen der Einheit*, 238-289.
[8] See "By-Laws of the Faith and Order Commission" in: Th. Best/G. Gassmann (eds.), *On the way to Fuller Koinonia: Official Report of the Fifth World Conference on Faith and Order* (Faith and Order Paper No.166), Geneva 1994, 309-313 ("Appendix V"). This document contains the text of the aim of the Faith and Order Commission. It also considers the Commission's functions, its organization, the world conferences, the meetings of the plenary and standing commission and the Faith and Order studies.

In 1952 the Commission organized the Third World Conference on Faith and Order in Lund (Sweden), where it moved from the former comparative method to a form of theological dialogue which seeks to bring out agreements and convergences, and to struggle with controversial issues by starting from a common biblical and christological basis. Of course, it is true that, as a frame of reference for the ecumenical discussion, a large amount of knowledge of the multicoloured character of the various traditions is indispensable. However, pinning oneself down to more or less fixed images and then comparing them to each other is quite another matter. Such a comparative fixation is always methodologically debatable and seems the best guarantee for the total failure of every ecumenical discussion from the very start. Every attempt to pin down an ecclesiastical tradition on a number of specific characteristics ignores the dynamics and diversity typical of every living tradition. One first entrenches oneself, as it were, only to subsequently discover that one has difficulty in looking across one's own parapet and that one can hardly catch sight of the other person. Hence the final report of Lund states:

> *"We have seen clearly that we can make no real advance in unity, if we only compare our several conceptions of the nature of the church and the traditions in which they are embodied"* [9].

In reaction to the so-called comparative ecclesiology a method of ecumenical discussion has presented itself within Faith and Order in which not the specific divergences, but the salient convergences are of primary importance. Within this method the mutual differences obviously also come up for discussion, but they are already classed under a certain heading, namely, that of convergences transcending mutual differences. The Lima text on baptism, eucharist and ministry is a good example of this method, which starts from these convergences, but at the same time does not gloss over the mutual differences [10].

---

[9] Cf. L. Vischer (ed.), *A Documentary History*, 85.
[10] Cf. for the method of convergence employed in the Lima text, e.g. M. Thurian/G. Wainwright (eds.), *Baptism and Eucharist. Ecumenical Convergence in Celebration* (Faith and Order Paper No. 117), Geneva 1983.

The Fourth World Conference of Faith and Order took place at Montreal (Canada) in 1963, during the period of the Second Vatican Council (1962-1965) and has especially become known for the formulation of a concept of tradition which shows a great measure of convergence with that of Vatican II.

The Fifth World Conference was held at Santiago de Compostela (Spain) in 1993 and dedicated to the theme "Towards Koinonia in Faith, Life and Witness". Here, with respect to strengthening the visible unity among the churches, the possibility was discussed of more explicit acknowledgments of baptism and of the debatability of the nature of historical episcopacy. The strongly Euro-American character of the work of Faith and Order was also recognized and a dialogue proposed which was to be more differentiated according to region. Finally, the interconnectedness of *fides et mores* (faith and morals) was more strongly emphasized: ethical questions are also questions of faith[11].

Since the Fourth World Assembly of the World Council of Churches at Uppsala (1968), the Roman Catholic Church has been officially represented by first 9, and now 15, members and participates in and supports all Faith and Order studies.

There is no doubt – to quote Gassmann once again – that Faith and Order has been and is an appropriate and effective instrument of and within the wider ecumenical movement. It has challenged and assisted the churches to overcome their doctrinal differences,

---

[11] Cf. for an assessment of the results of Santiago, B. Hoedemaker/ A. Houtepen/ Th. Witvliet, *Oecumene als leerproces. Inleiding in de oecumenica*, Zoetermeer 1993, 253-264. See further M. Parmentier, "Die fünfte Weltkonferenz der Commission für Glauben und Kirchenverfassung, Santiago de Compostela, August 1993", *Internationale Kirchliche Zeitschrift* 84 (1994) 156-180 and M. Gosker, "The Fifth World Conference on Faith and Order, Santiago de Compostela", *One in Christ* 24 (1993) 318-327. The connection between the work of Faith and Order and Church and Society (the continuation of Life and Work) was, in particular, articulated in the report of Th.F. Best/W. Granberg-Michaelson (eds.), *Costly Unity: Koinonia and Justice, Peace and Creation*, Geneva 1993. See for the texts of Santiago, *Fifth World Conference on Faith and Order Santiago de Compostela 1993: Message-Section Reports-Discussion Paper* (Faith and Order Paper No. 164), Geneva 1993 and Th.Best/G. Gassmann, *On the way to Fuller Koinonia*.

to share their diverse spiritual and theological insights and forms of life as a source of mutual enrichment and renewal, and to reappropriate and express together their common heritage in faith, life and witness.

All these efforts have as their goal the manifestation of the visible unity of the church of Jesus Christ[12]. This goal is seen in the wider perspective of the calling of the churches, sustained and inspired by the Holy Spirit, to become a credible sign and instrument of God's saving and transforming purpose for all humanity and creation[13].

The literature on the Faith and Order movement can be divided into three categories:

In the first place, there is the general literature on the problems of faith and order: those writings and statements of individual theologians which have an important bearing on the question of church unity, and the reports of meetings and conferences of individual groups who have worked together on a specific subject in its relation to unity in Christ. These writings and reports have

---

[12] See for a historical survey, P. Crow/G. Gassmann, *Lausanne 1927 to Santiago de Compostela: The Faith and Order World Conferences, and Issues and Results of the Working Period 1963-1993* (Faith and Order Paper No.160), Geneva 1993. Cf. also H. Döring, *Kirchen – unterwegs zur Einheit: Das Ringen um die sichtbare Einheit der Kirchen in den Dokumenten der Weltkirchenkonferenzen*, München/Paderborn/Wien 1969 and A. Houtepen, "Zichtbare eenheid in zicht?" in: Idem (red.), *Gerechtigheid, Eenheid en Vrede: De oecumenische agenda van de Wereldraadbijeenkomst te Vancouver 1983*, Amersfoort-Voorburg 1982, 58-76 and Idem, "De Heilige Geest en de zichtbare eenheid van de kerk" in: M.E. Brinkman (red.), *'Kom Heilige Geest, vernieuw de hele schepping': 12 Nederlandse commentaren bij internationale oecumenische ontwikkelingen met het oog op de zevende assemblee van de Wereldraad van Kerken te Canberra, Australië, 7-20 febr., 1991*, Voorburg 1990, 33-49.

[13] See for the church as "the sign of the coming unity of mankind", N. Goodall (ed.), *The Uppsala Report 1968: Official Report of the Fourth Assembly of the World Council of Churches Uppsala July 4-20, 1968*, Geneva 1968, 17. This phrase deliberately alludes to the expression in *Lumen Gentium*, No.1 that the Church in Christ and in the nature of sacrament is "a sign and instrument of communion with God and of unity among all men". See for the English translation of the texts of Vatican II, A. Flannery (ed.), *Vatican Council II: The Conciliar and Post Conciliar Documents*, Dublin 1975. See for the Dutch Text *Constituties & Decreten van het 2e Vaticaans oecumenisch concilie*, Leusden 1986 and for the Latin text *Conciliorum Oecumenicorum Decreta*, Bologna 1973[3].

often had an indirect or direct influence on the work of Faith and Order.

A second more specific category of literature is directly connected with a world conference. There is, first, the preparatory material and there is, secondly, the report proper.

A third category is the literature which concerns itself with the results of a conference or a series of conferences. It consists of articles, essays and historical surveys.

In this study we will concentrate on the second and third category of literature.

The Ecclesiological Debate within Faith and Order

Fundamental to the ecumenical self-understanding of Faith and Order is the ecclesiological point of departure which was adopted by the Central Committee at Toronto in 1950, shortly after the foundation of the World Council in 1948. Obviously, within a very short time, misunderstandings about the World Council's intentions had arisen. This should not cause any surprise, for the World Council represents indeed a new and unprecedented approach to the problem of inter-church relationships. Therefore, its purpose and nature can be easily misunderstood. In the so-called Toronto Statement, an attempt is made to eliminate a great number of these misunderstandings. First, there is a clear statement of what the World Council does not intend. This is followed by a statement of its aims. The result is an outspokenness and clarity which is striking in ecumenical circles, and which deserves to be quoted in extenso:

> "*1. The World Council of Churches is not and must never become a Super-Church*.
> *It is not a Super-Church. It is not the World Church. It is not the Una Sancta of which the Creeds speak. This misunderstanding arises again and again although it has been denied as clearly as possible in official pronouncements of the Council. It is based on complete ignorance of the real situation within the Council. For if the Council should in any way violate its own constitutional prin-*

ciple, that it cannot legislate or act for its member Churches, it would cease to maintain the support of its membership.

2. The purpose of the World Council of Churches is not to negotiate unions between Churches, which can only be done by the Churches themselves acting on their own initiative, but to bring the Churches into living contact with each other and to promote the study and discussion of the issues of Church unity.

By its very existence and its activities the Council bears witness to the necessity of a clear manifestation of the oneness of the Church of Christ. But it remains the right and duty of each Church to draw from its ecumenical experience such consequences as it feels bound to do on the basis of its own convictions. No Church, therefore, need fear that the Council will press it into decisions concerning union with other Churches.

3. The World Council cannot and should not be based on any one particular conception of the Church. It does not prejudge the ecclesiological problem.

It is often suggested that the dominating or underlying conception of the Council is that of such and such a Church or such and such a school of theology. It may well be that at a certain particular conference or in a particular utterance one can find traces of the strong influence of a certain tradition or theology.

*The Council as such cannot possibly become the instrument of one confession or school without losing its very **raison d'être**. There are room and space in the World Council for the ecclesiology of every Church which is ready to participate in the ecumenical conversation and which takes its stand on the Basis of the Council, which is 'a fellowship of Churches which accept our Lord Jesus Christ as God and Saviour'.*

The World Council exists in order that different Churches may face their differences, and therefore no Church is obliged to change its ecclesiology as a consequence of membership in the World Council.

4. Membership in the World Council of Churches does not imply that a Church treats its own conception of the Church as merely relative.

There are critics, and not infrequently friends, of the ecumenical movement who criticize or praise it for its alleged inherent latitudinarianism. According to them the ecumenical movement stands for the fundamental equality of all Christian doctrines and conceptions of the Church and is, therefore, not concerned with the question of truth. This misunderstanding is due to the fact that ecumenism has in the minds of these persons become identified with certain particular theories about unity, which have played a role in ecumenical history, but which do not represent the common view of the movement as a whole, and have never been officially endorsed by the World Council.

5. Membership in the World Council does not imply the acceptance of a specific doctrine concerning the nature of Church unity.
The Council stands for Church unity. But in its midst there are those who conceive unity wholly or largely as a full consensus in the realm of doctrine, other who conceive of it primarily as sacramental communion based on common church order, others who consider both indispensable, others who would only require unity in certain fundamentals of faith and order, again others who conceive the one Church exclusively as a universal spiritual fellowship, or hold that visible unity is inessential or even undesirable. But none of these conceptions can be called the ecumenical theory. The whole point of the ecumenical conversation is precisely that all these conceptions enter into dynamic relations with each other. (...)".

Besides these five 'negative points' the Toronto Statement also mentions eight positive points, two of which, the third and the fifth proposition, are quite essential, especially with a view to the relation with the Roman Catholic Church[14]:

"3. The member Churches recognize that the membership of the Church of Christ is more inclusive than the membership of their

---

[14] Cf. J.J. Mc Donnell, *The World Council of Churches and the Catholic Church* (Toronto Studies in Theology, Vol.21), New York-Toronto 1985, 225-232 and L. Vischer, "The Ecumenical Movement and the Roman Catholic Church" in: H.E. Fey (ed.), *The Ecumenical Advance: A History of the Ecumenical Movement*, Vol.II: 1948-1968, London 1970, 311-352. See on the issue of possible Roman Catholic membership of the World Council of Churches the report of the Joint Working Group "Patterns of Relationships between the Roman Catholic Church and the World Council of Churches", *The Ecumenical Review* 24 (1972) 247-288 and for the ongoing discussion on this theme A. Houtepen, "Towards Conciliar Collaboration: the WCC and the Roman Catholic Communion of Churches", *The Ecumenical Review* 40 (1988) 473-487 (with many references to the relevant literature) and J. Willebrands, "Veertig jaar Wereldraad van Kerken; een katholieke reflectie", *Kosmos en Oekumene* 22 (1988) 184-191.

own Church body. They seek, therefore, to enter into living con-
tact with those outside their own ranks who confess the Lordship
of Christ.
All the Christian Churches, including the Church of Rome, hold
that there is no complete identity between the membership of the
Church Universal and the membership of their own Church. They
recognize that there are Church members **extra muros***, that these*
belong **aliquo modo** *to the Church, or even that there is an* **eccle-**
sia extra ecclesiam*. This recognition finds expression in the fact*
that with very few exceptions the Christian Churches accept the
baptism administered by other Churches as valid.

5. **The member Churches of the World Council recognize in**
other Churches elements of the true Church. They consider that
this mutual recognition obliges them to enter into a serious con-
versation with each other in the hope that these elements of truth
will lead to the recognition of the full truth and to unity based on
the full truth.
It is generally taught in the different Churches that other Churches
have certain elements of the true Church, in some traditions called
vestigia ecclesiae*. Such elements are the preaching of the Word,*
the teaching of the Holy Scriptures, and the administration of the
sacraments. These elements are more than pale shadows of the life
of the true Church. They are a fact of real promise and provide an
opportunity to strive by frank and brotherly intercourse for the
realization of a fuller unity. Moreover, Christians of all ecclesio-
logical views throughout the world, by the preaching of the
Gospel, brought men and women to salvation by Christ, to new-
ness of life in Him, and into Christian fellowship with one
another" [15].

In a great many texts of Vatican II we find in a certain sense the
indirect answers to the theses of Toronto. The theme of the *vestigia
ecclesiae*, made familiar by the Toronto Statement, was picked up
not only in *Lumen Gentium*, No. 15 which even speaks of Christians in some real way joined to us in the Holy Spirit (*quaedam in
Spiritu Sancto coniunctio*), but above all in *Unitatis Redintegratio*,
No. 3 and No. 22. The latter document employs the more positive
terms "bona" and "elementa" as well as the extremely interesting

---

[15] See for the so-called Toronto Statement, L. Vischer (ed.), *A Documentary History*, 167-176, esp. 169-171, 172 and 174.

concept of incomplete communion. This concept certainly does not put the churches on a par with each other, but it does set them within one and the same Christian economy, within which ecumenism is seeking to establish complete communion.

The expression that the Church of Christ subsists in the Catholic Church (*subsistit in ecclesia catholica*) in *Lumen Gentium*, No. 8, which is picked up in *Unitatis Redintegratio*, No. 4 and in *Dignitatis Humanae*, No. 1, permits the assertion that the Church of Christ and of the Apostles exists in the Roman Catholic Church, while not excluding the idea that others, too, are in some sense 'Church'. This was the response of the Vatican Council to the Toronto Statement's plea 'not to unchurch' the others[16].

It is on the basis of this acknowledgment of each other's being church that the ecumenical movement lives. Taking this as its point of departure, the ecumenical movement moves towards a growing recognition and acknowledgment of the various churches being totally church. This acknowledgment can only arise there where all churches view themselves as having a communio (koinonia) relation to Jesus Christ which transcends and regulates every concrete form of church communion.

The Concept of Koinonia

Real *koinonia* in the life of the Father, the Son and the Holy Spirit (cf. John 14,17; I John 1,2-10; II Pet. 1,4; I Cor. 1,9 en II Cor. 13,13) – as the Faith and Order Commission states – is the life centre of all who confess Jesus Christ as Lord and Saviour. They share and participate in the gospel and in the apostolic faith, in suffering and in service (II Cor.8,4; Rom.15,26 and Acts 2,32). This *koinonia* is lived in Christ through baptism (Rom.6,1-14) and the eucharist (I Cor.11,17-34) and in the community with its pastors and guides (Heb.13,1-7).

---

[16] Cf. Y. Congar, "Fifty Years in Quest of Unity" in: *Lausanne 77: Fifty Years of Faith and Order* (Faith and Order Paper, No. 82), Geneva 1977, 21-37.

Koinonia means, in addition, participation in the holy things of God and the communion of the saints of all times and places (*communio sanctorum* in the double sense of the word). Each local Christian community is related in *koinonia* with all other local Christian communities with whom it shares the same faith. In this *koinonia* they live the catholicity of the church[17]. In the concept of *koinonia* there are several dimensions which makes it especially useful for ecumenical ecclesiology[18].

In the first place, in the current ecumenical ecclesiological debates *koinonia* functions as a concept of synthesis. It is not an alternative to any of the New Testament images and metaphors for the Church. Rather, *koinonia* pulls together the basic threads of such images. Since *koinonia* is regarded as a comprehensive category, it is not surprising that it is used to express the quintessence of the Church. *Koinonia* means that the visible bond with God that, at the same time, is the bond of the new community, is the sign and the instrument of God's reconciling purpose. Therefore, *koinonia* indicates the intimate connection between salvation and the Church. The reality of salvation in Christ is anything but abstract or individualistic. Since this reality is fundamentally indivisible, it is communal and therefore ecclesial.

Secondly, while denoting fundamental unity, the notion of communion at the same time opens up a constructive approach to diversity. *Koinonia* is not an all-or-nothing proposition. It is a dynamic notion because it allows one to speak of growing in the communion one shares already. Therefore, it admits of degrees. Hence, the Second Vatican Council could say that between the Roman Catholic Church and the separated churches or ecclesial communities "a certain but imperfect communion exists". The recognition of this reality opens the way for working towards greater unity, without demanding uniformity[19].

---

[17] *Baptism, Eucharist & Ministry 1982-1990*, 150.
[18] See esp. J.M.R. Tillard, *Église d'Églises. L'écclésiologie de communion*, Paris 1987.
[19] Cf. G. Vandervelde, "Koinonia Ecclesiology – Ecumenical Breakthrough?", *One in Christ* 29 (1993) 126-142. See also *Fifth World Conference on Faith and*

Catholicity and Apostolicity

Thus, in the concept of koinonia the catholicity and apostolocity of the church of all times and all places meet. The Church is catholic in its being, in its being in Christ. Where Jesus Christ is, there, too, is the Church catholic, in which, in all ages, the Holy Spirit makes people participants of Christ's life and salvation, without respect of sex, race and position. In each local church the fullness of grace and truth is present. Hence, real catholicity requires the communion of all local churches and pertains to the identity of each local church and constitutes an essential quality of their communion together. "This is the standpoint from which we see catholicity" – as the Louvain report stated in 1971 –: "trinitarian, christocentric, pneumatic, missionary and demanding a concrete engagement in the service of mankind"[20].

Moreover, in the Lima text the World Council of Churches gives the following definition of apostolicity:

> "Apostolic tradition in the Church means continuity in the permanent characteristics of the Church of the apostles: witness to the apostolic faith, proclamation and fresh interpretation of the Gospel, celebration of baptism and the eucharist, the transmission of ministerial responsibilities, communion in prayer, love, joy and suffering, service to the sick and the needy, unity among the local churches and sharing the gifts which the Lord has given to each"[21].

Order Santiago de Compostela 1993: Message-Section Reports-Discussion Paper, 7 where the "interdependence of unity and diversity" is called "the essence of the Church's koinonia". Cf. Th.F. Best/G. Gassmann (ed.), On the way to Fuller Koinonia, 231.

[20] Cf. the report "Catholicity and Apostolicity" in: Faith and Order Louvain 1971: Study Reports and Documents (Faith and Order Paper No. 59), Geneva 1971, 133-168, esp. 136-140. This report has been written on behalf of the Joint Working Group between the Roman Catholic Church and the World Council of Churches. See also for the text of this document and the preparatory papers of R. Schnackenburg, J.N.D. Kelly, E. Lanne, J.D. Zizioulas, J. Bosc, A. Ganoczy, J. Witte and W. Pannenberg One in Christ 6 (1970) No.3. Cf. further the report of Section I on "The Holy Spirit and the Catholicity of the Church" in: N. Goodall (ed.), The Uppsala Report 1968: Official Report of the Fourth Assembly of the World Council of Churches Uppsala July 4-20,1968, Geneva 1968, 11-18.

[21] Cf. Baptism, Eucharist and Ministry, Geneva 1982, 28 (M.34).

According to this definition of apostolicity its content is primarily a matter of continuity in witness, proclamation, celebration, service and sharing of gifts[22]. As such it is a "critical concept in reference to which the faith, life and structure of the Church are to be repeatedly measured and oriented"[23]. On the basis of this critical function of the concept of apostolicity, it will also be clear that a distinction should be made between the apostolic tradition of the whole church and the succession of the apostolic ministry. The primary manifestation of apostolic succession is to be found in the apostolic tradition of the Church as a whole. The succession is an expression of the permanence and, therefore, of the continuity of Christ's own mission in which the Church participates. Within the Church the ordained ministry has a particular task of preserving and actualizing the apostolic faith[24].

Whether episcopal succession is the most adequate expression of apostolic succession and continuity is now at the centre of the

---

[22] Cf. G. Vandervelde, "The Meaning of 'Apostolic Faith' in World Council of Churches' Documents" in: Th. Horgan (ed.), *Apostolic Faith in America*, Grand Rapids 1988, 20-25, esp. 22/23. On the basis of the Joint Working Group Report "Catholicity and Apostolicity" (*Faith and Order Louvain 1971*, 138-140), he discerns seven aspects of the concept of apostolicity:
1. *Foundation*: The church is built upon the foundation of the apostles.
2. *Continuity*: The Holy Spirit that the apostles received continues to act in the church.
3. *Variegated Task*: In view of the multifaceted tasks fulfilled by the apostles, the apostolicity of the church is credible only as it faithfully assumes this variety of tasks.
4. *Mission*: It is in virtue of its *participation in the mission* of Christ in the mission of disciples that the Church is apostolic.
5. *Hope*: Because the kingdom is to be fully realized at the end of time, apostolicity includes an intimate and essential link with the final accomplishment of God's saving plan.
6. *Memory*: The memory of the church embraces all the past which is constantly actualized in the Word and the Sacraments.
7. *Diversity of Ministries*: The Church is apostolic because it continues faithfully the mission, the preaching and the ministry which it has received from the Apostles.
[23] Cf. *Fifth World Conference on Faith and Order Santiago de Compostela. Message-Section Reports-Discussion Paper*, 16 and Th.F. Best/G. Gassmann (ed.), *On the way to Fuller Koinonia*, 239.
[24] *Baptism, Eucharist and Ministry*, 28/29 (M.35 and the Commentary on M.34).

ecumenical discussion on ministry. In any case, there is a growing agreement in ecumenical dialogues that the apostolicity or apostolic tradition of the Church is broader than the concept of apostolic succession of ministry[25].

When the World Council of Churches articulates its goal in terms of 'conciliar fellowship', the term needs to be understood as this kind of catholic and apostolic *koinonia* among local Churches. Hence, the Fifth World Assembly at Nairobi (1975), referring to what was already formulated at the Third World Assembly at New Delhi (1961), declares:

> "*The one Church is to be envisioned as a conciliar fellowship of local churches which are themselves truly united. In this conciliar fellowship, each local church possesses, in communion with the others, the fullness of catholicity, witnesses to the same apostolic faith, and therefore recognizes the others as belonging to the same Church of Christ and guided by the same Spirit. As the New Delhi Assembly pointed out, they are bound together because they have received the same baptism and share in the same Eucharist; they recognize each other's members and ministries. They are one in their common commitment to confess the gospel of Christ by proclamation and service to the world. To this end, each church aims at maintaining sustained and sustaining relationships with her sister churches, expressed in conciliar gatherings whenever required for the fulfilment of their common calling*" [26].

---

[25] Cf. *Confessing the One Faith: An Ecumenical Explication of the Apostolic Faith as it is Confessed in the Nicene-Constantinopolitan Creed (381)* (Faith and Order Paper No. 153), Geneva 1991, 89/90: "The various traditions differ in their understanding of *apostolic succession*. Some put the emphasis on succession in apostolic teaching. Others combine this with the recognition of an ordered transmission of the ministry of word and sacrament. Others again understand apostolic succession primarily as the unbroken succession of episcopal ordinations".

[26] Cf. G. Gassmann (ed.), *Documentary History*, 3. See on the meaning of the term 'conciliar fellowship' in relation to 'local churches' the Salamanca report (1973) "The Unity of the Church – Next Steps" in: *Ibid.*, 35-49, esp. 37-40. In the emphasis on the central meaning of the witness of the Scriptures, the one baptism, the one eucharist, the common apostolic faith and the mutual recognition of ministries for the unity of the Church, traces are easily recognized of the old so-called Lambeth Quadrilateral of the Anglican Church, dating from 1888, about the basic elements of every form of church communion. See C. Buchanan on the "Lambeth Quadrilateral" in N. Lossky et al. (ed.), *Dictionary of the Ecumenical Movement*, 586. See also B. Hoedemaker/A. Houtepen/Th. Witvliet, *Oecumene als leerproces*, 200.

The New Delhi text mentioned here reads as follows:

> "We believe that the unity which is both God's will and his gift to
> his Church is being made visible as all in each place who are bap-
> tized into Jesus Christ and confess him as Lord and Saviour are
> brought by the Holy Spirit into one fully committed fellowship,
> holding the one apostolic faith, preaching the one Gospel, break-
> ing the one bread, joining in common prayer, and having a corpo-
> rate life reaching out in witness and service to all and who at the
> same time are united with the whole Christian fellowship in all
> places and all ages in such wise that ministry and members are
> accepted by all, and that all can act and speak together as occa-
> sion requires for the tasks to which God calls his people" [27].

Fellowship of Local Churches

This emphasis on the communio of local churches[28] in which
the full catholicity of the church of Christ is present is not something typical of the World Council of Churches. It is also found in
texts of Vatican II such as, for example, *Lumen Gentium*, No. 26,
and *Christus Dominus*, No. 22:

> "This Church of Christ is really present in all legitimately orga-
> nized local groups of the faithful, which, in so far as they are
> united to their pastors, are also quite appropriately called

---

[27] G. Gassmann (ed.), *Documentary History*, 3.

[28] The meaning of the term "local church" is not the same in all confessional traditions. Three broad types may be distinguished:
1. The local church is the Church under the leadership of a bishop.
2. The local church is the Church under the leadership of a presbyter.
3. The local church is the gathered community.
The first type is the result of the expansion of the early church. The bishop, originally presiding over the one community which existed in a given place, now has
responsibility for several communities; these communities are still regarded as one
community. The second type represents a further stage. The role originally played
by the bishop has now in part been attributed to the presbyter. The third type is the
result of the rediscovery of the charismatic community, often with a strong element
of rebellion against hierarchical or political interference and pressure.
Cf. for a description of these different types the text of the Geneva report (1976)
on "A Fellowship of Local Churches Truly United" in: G. Gassmann (ed.), *Documentary History*, 69-75, esp. 71/72.

Churches in the New Testament. For these are in fact, in their own localities, the new people called by God, in the power of the Holy Spirit and as result of full conviction (cf. I Thess. 1:5)".
"For a diocese to fulfill its purpose it is necessary that the nature of the Church be clearly manifested in the People of God belonging to the diocese".

Hence, the Joint Working group between the Roman Catholic Church and the World Council of Churches, in a study document on "The Church: Local and Universal", arrives at an extensive degree of agreement on the following points:

1. The local church is truly church.

2. The local church is not an administrative or juridical subsection or part of the universal church.

3. All Christian World Communions can, in general, agree with the definition of the local church as a community of baptized believers in which the word of God is preached, the apostolic faith confessed, the sacraments are celebrated, the redemptive work of Christ for the world is witnessed to, and a ministry of *episcope* exercised by bishops or other ministers is serving the community. Differences between the World Communions are connected with the role and place of the bishop in relation to the local church[29].

This recognition and acknowledgment of the complete church in the various local churches has especially been stimulated by the New Testament concept of koinonia. On the basis of this concept it becomes clear that every church that baptizes in the name of the Father, the Son and the Holy Spirit and conforms to the apostolic proclamation as handed down to us in Holy Scripture, already participates in this communion. Indeed, one can see here an instance of a real, albeit incomplete, union of the Christian churches, which also manifests itself already in each separate church[30].

---

[29] Cf. *Joint Working Group between the Roman Catholic Church and the World Council of Churches: Sixth Report including two Study Documents*, Geneva-Rome 1990, 23-37, esp. 27/28.
[30] See for the role of the koinonia concept in recent ecumenical dialogues the study of the Institute for Ecumenical Research in Strasbourg *Communio/Koinonia. A New Testament-Early Christian Concept and its Contemporary Appropriation and Significance*, Strasbourg 1990.

It is remarkable, however, that the World Assembly at Nairobi (1975), far more expressly than the World Assembly at New Delhi (1961) and at Uppsala (1968)[31], distinguishes between conciliarity as an attitude towards a future universal council and conciliarity as a sign of unity. While the latter form of conciliarity does not yet exist, a form of anticipation of this genuine conciliarity does already exist:

> "*Our present interconfessional assemblies are not councils in this full sense, because they are not yet united by a common understanding of the apostolic faith, by a common ministry, and a common Eucharist. They nevertheless express the sincere desire of the participating churches to herald and move towards full conciliar fellowship, and are themselves a true foretaste of such fellowship*"[32].

In fact, a type of opposition becomes manifest here which was later to manifest itself around intercommunion (see chapter V). Then it concerns the question of whether real conciliarity or real intercommunion may be a means towards future unity or only a sign, in the sense of an expression, of existing unity. Eastern-Orthodoxy especially, and, in a somewhat mitigated form, the Roman Catholic Church, take the latter view[33].

This distinction manifested itself already in the Bristol report (1967) on "The Importance of the Conciliar Process in the Ancient Church". There it is argued that the conciliar process in

---

[31] Cf. N. Goodall (ed.), *The Uppsala Report 1968*, 11-19 ("The Holy Spirit and the Catholicity of the Church"), esp. 17: "In a time when human interdependence is so evident, it is the more imperative to make visible the bonds which unite Christians in universal fellowship. .... The ecumenical movement helps to enlarge this experience of universality, and its regional councils and its World Council may be regarded as a transitional opportunity for eventually actualizing a truly universal, ecumenical, conciliar form of common life and witness".

[32] Cf. D.M. Paton (ed.), *Breaking Barriers Nairobi 1975: The Official Report of the Fifth Assembly of the World Council of Churches, Nairobi, 23 November-10 December,1975*, London-Grand Rapids 1976, 59-70, esp. 61.

[33] See for an Orthodox approach, D. Popescu, "The Local Church and Conciliar Fellowship", *The Ecumenical Review* 29 (1977) 265-272, esp. 268 and, for a Roman Catholic approach, B. Hearne, "Conciliar Fellowship and the Local Church: A Catholic View from Africa", *The Ecumenical Review* 29 (1977) 129-140.

the ancient church took place on the basis of the existing fellowship, but that the present point of departure is one of plural ecclesiastical communities in confrontation with one another. Since the
unity of the Church is the presupposition for holding an Ecumenical Council, an assembly which is called by separated churches
which do not live in eucharistic fellowship can decisively advance
unity, but cannot be designated as a council. For – so the report
stresses – eucharistic fellowship must be the starting-point.

That does not mean, however, – so the report puts its own strict
standpoint in the proper perspective – that the division and differences must be fully overcome. Councils were often held precisely
when the eucharistic fellowship was most seriously jeopardized and
the signs of rupture were clearly visible. Precisely through posing a
burning question, a council can bring churches together. However,
this acceptance of conciliarity is bound to one clear condition: a
council as a means towards unity can only take place when it speaks
and acts out of an at least potentially present eucharistic fellowship[34].

In the report "Conciliarity and the Future of the Ecumenical
Movement", presented in Louvain in 1971, it is still clearer that in
the World Council of Churches there are two concepts of conciliarity, namely conciliarity in the full sense of the word and conciliarity in the derived sense of the word. In the derived sense of the
word, the report states that conciliarity has been, in some form or
degree, characteristic of the life of the Christian Church in all ages
and at various levels:

> *"By conciliarity we mean the coming together of Christians –
> locally, regionally or globally – for common prayer, counsel
> and decision, in the belief that the Holy Spirit can use such
> meetings for his own purpose of reconciling, renewing and
> reforming the Church by guiding it towards the fullness of truth
> and love"[35].*

However, it is clear that the councils which have been created
as expressions of the ecumenical movement in our time do not

[34] See for the text of this report, G. Gassmann (ed.), *Documentary History*, 209-
217, esp. 216/217.
[35] See for the text of the report, *Ibid.*, 236-239, esp. 236.

possess the fullness of conciliarity as it is to be seen in the great
Councils of the early Church. The reason for this deficiency is not
in the first place their lack of universality. The central fact in true
conciliarity is the active presence and work of the Holy Spirit
leading to acceptance of its decisions by the Church as fully
authoritative. This true conciliarity has always been marked by or
has led to full eucharistic fellowship.

In spite of this clear distinction, the report nevertheless raises a
great number of questions which have accompanied the ecumenical movement up to now: What are the pre-conditions for a true
council? Could there be a 'reunion Council' which did not presuppose eucharistic fellowship and full consensus, but accepted
the search for and the expectation of these as gifts of the Holy
Spirit? These questions, as well as many other questions regarding the nature of representation and the role of bishops in a council, require study, so the report states. As a conclusion the report,
however, formulates a standpoint that comes close to the concept
of conciliarity as a means. The present World Council of
Churches and other similar regional and local councils are "*meeting places*" for churches which are not yet in full communion
and do not yet accept a common authority. They do nevertheless
provide a "*framework*" within which true conciliarity can
develop. Inasmuch as they are guided and inspired by the Holy
Spirit they have – if only in an anticipatory form – the character
of conciliarity[36].

In the present situation of the ecumenical movement there is no
further clarification of this term. Thus, up to now, the term 'conciliar' has implied a reference either to a "*process*" by which the
churches work towards unity, or to an "*event*" which expresses a
unity which has already been achieved[37]. Against the background

---

[36] *Ibid.*, 238.
[37] Cf. A. Keshishian, *Conciliar Fellowship: A Common Goal*, Geneva 1992, 2-5,
esp. 4 who distinguishes no fewer than five meanings in current ecumenical
usage:
"1. The term conciliarity is used in the ecumenical debate in a rather imprecise and
ambiguous way. It is also employed interchangeably with conciliar fellowship.

of this distinction, the Salamanca report on "The Unity of the Church – Next Steps" (1973) calls the World Council of Churches and the National Councils of Churches, as instruments to promote the search for unity, *"preconciliar"*[38].

A Comprehensive Approach to Different Church Traditions

This unity can be further developed with the help of different key conceptions and images which have been especially emphasized by different Christian traditions. Together they could contribute in a complementary way to an ecumenically oriented ecclesiology of *koinonia*. In the report on the responses of the churches to the Lima text, the Faith and Order Commission sums up four key conceptions of the church:

> "*a*) **The church a s gift of the word of God (creatura verbi)**
>
> *The koinonia of the church is centred and grounded in the word of God testified in the scriptures, incarnated in Jesus Christ and visible among us through the living voice of the gospel in preaching, in sacraments and in service. Alle church institutions, forms of ministry, liturgical expressions and methods of mission should be submitted to the word of God and tested by it. The* **pleroma** *of God's creative word is never exhausted in the churches' institutions.*
>
> *b)* **The church as mystery or sacrament of God's love for the world**
>
> *The church as* **koinonia** *is the church of the living God (I Tim. 3:15), not a human association only. It lives in permanent com-*

2. Conciliarity may point to an essential *feature* of the church's nature and an important *pattern* of its common life.

3. It may imply both the *fellowship* of divided churches (*conseil*) and the *representative gathering* of the one church (*concile*).

4. It may point both to the ultimate *goal* of unity and to the *means* towards this goal.

5. It may refer to the *form* as well as to the *vision* of church unity".

See for a Protestant (Calvinist) assessment of the use of the term conciliarity in the World Council of Churches, J. Veenhof, "Pluraliteit en Conciliariteit" in: J.M. Vlijm (ed.), *Geloofsmanieren. Studies over pluraliteit in de kerk*, Kampen 1981, 168-197.

[38] Cf. G. Gassmann (ed.), *Documentary History*, 38.

munion with God the Father through Jesus Christ in the Holy Spirit and is not merely the historical product of Jesus' ministry. .... Therefore the visible organizational structures of the church must always be seen in the light of God's gifts of salvation in Christ. The word and the sacraments of Jesus Christ are forms of God's real and saving presence for the world. As such they express the church's participation in the mystery of Christ and are inseparable from it.

c) The church as the pilgrim people of God

*A third aspect of the understanding of the church as **koinonia** stresses the provisional and incomplete character of the church in its present form, its hope and despair, its suffering and compassion, its shame and glory, its being still a mixed reality of sinners and saints. The church is a community of justified sinners in search of the kingdom of God, struggling as they serve the world to be obedient to the commands and promises of Christ as expressed in the sermon on the mount. It is a community of pilgrims who have already received a foretaste of that fulfilment for which they are longing.*

d) The church as servant and prophetic sign of God's coming kingdom

The church is also a servant people for God's coming kingdom, 'the sign held up before the nations'. As a first-fruit of the kingdom the church takes sides with the weak, the poor and the alienated. This for the sake of involving all its members in a personal appeal to seek first of all the kingdom of God by being itself, as a collective whole, an instrument for the liberation of people in distress. An ecumenically conceived ecclesiology, therefore, must not be self-centred, triumphalistic or complacent, but should direct the churches' service to the world, to justice, peace and integrity of creation"[39].

Since all these concepts and images belong to the common biblical heritage and are found in the apostolic tradition, there is hope that these complementary approaches will lead to a convergent vision on the nature, unity and mission of the church.

If ecclesiology is seen as the legitimation of the institutions of the divided confessions, then the four models would, at their

---

[39] Cf. *Baptism, Eucharist & Ministry 1982-1990*, 150/151.

extremes, exclude one another. Sheer sacramentalism or a merely hierarchical view of the church could hardly be reconciled, within one communion, with a prophetic critique of sacerdotalism.

However, if ecclesiology could be seen as the reflection on the essential characteristics or structures of the Church of God and on its given unity as a gift and a calling from God and as a human responsibility of love and service among Christ's followers; if ecclesiology were taken to mean giving account of our hope (I Peter 3:15)[40] and the search for the credibility of our faith; if it meant pneumatology, christology, soteriology, eschatology 'in action', then we would be witnesses of an ecumenical ecclesiology which sought the unity of the Church 'that the world might believe'[41].

Such a common ecclesiology will be decisive for Christian identity in the pluralist and secularising world of the next decades. It is already decisive today for the hope and faith of millions who, hungry and dying, are looking for the 'signal hoisted for the nations': *Lumen Gentium*?[42]

A real *koinonia* ecclesiology can function as a catalyst, but new formulations and statements, as such, will not trigger the much-needed breakthrough to greater unity. A breakthrough will more likely be sparked off by stories of the gospel drama of lived *koinonia*: the stories of communities of various traditions that – in the destitution of Somalia, or in the crucible of Bosnia, or in the chaos of Russia, or in the moral-spiritual void in Europe and North America, or in the grinding poverty in the streets of Washington or Manila – experience anew the *koinonia* of the one Body of Christ.

[40] See on the WCC study project, "Giving Account of the Hope within us", G. Gassmann (ed.), *A Documentary History*, 161-170.

[41] See for such a similar complementary approach of the different 'models' of the church, A. Dulles, S.J., *Models of the Church: A Critical Assessent of the Church in all its Aspects*, Dublin 1976, who distinguishes five predominant church models: the church as institution, as mystical communion, as sacrament, as herald and as servant.

[42] Cf. A. Houtepen, "Towards an Ecumenical Vision of the Church", *One in Christ* 25 (1989) 217-237, esp. 234 and 237.

Careful, expectant, prayerful listening to the Lord of history and the Church, through the stories of his people, can become the means by which the Spirit of *koinonia* brings about a deepened and embodied *koinonia* of the Spirit[43].

At the end of this short survey of the ecclesiological debate within Faith and Order I would like to quote, as a kind of conclusion, some of the main phrases in the statement on unity of the Seventh World Assembly of the World Council of Churches in Canberra (1991) on the "Calling of the Church", on 'the Unity of the Church to which we are called" and on "the Challenge at this Moment in the Ecumenical Movement":

> *"1.2 The calling of the Church is to proclaim reconciliation and provide healing, to overcome divisions based on race, gender, age, culture, colour, and to bring all people into communion with God. Because of sin and the misunderstanding of the diverse gifts of the Spirit, the churches are painfully divided within themselves and among each other. The scandalous divisions damage the credibility of their witness to the world in worship and service. Moreover they contradict not only the church's witness but also its very nature.*
>
> *2.1. The unity of the church to which we are called is a koinonia given and expressed in the common confession of the apostolic faith; a common sacramental life entered by the one baptism and celebrated together in one eucharistic fellowship; a common life in which members and ministries are mutually recognized and reconciled; and a common mission witnessing to the gospel of God's grace to all people and serving the whole creation. The goal of the search for full communion is realized when all the churches are able to recognize in one another the one, holy, catholic and apostolic church in its fullness. This full communion will be expressed on the local and the universal levels through conciliar forms of life and action. In such communion churches are bound in all aspects of their life together at all levels in confessing the one faith and engaging in worship and witness, deliberation and action.*
>
> *3.2. The challenge at this moment in the ecumenical movement as a reconciling and renewing movement towards full visible unity is ... to call all churches:*

---

[43] Cf. G. Vandervelde, "Koinonia Ecclesiology – Ecumenical Breakthrough?", 142.

– *to recognize each other's baptism on the basis of the BEM document;*
– *to move towards the recognition of the apostolic faith as
expressed through the Nicene-Constantinopolitan Creed in the life
and witness of one another;*
– *on the basis of convergence in faith in baptism, eucharist and
ministry to consider, wherever appropriate, forms of eucharistic
hospitality ...;*
– *to move towards a mutual recognition of ministries;*
– *to endeavour in word and deed to give common witness to the
gospel as a whole;*
– *to recommit themselves to work for justice, peace and integrity
of creation, linking more closely the search for the sacramental
communion of the church with the struggles for justice and peace;*
– *to help parishes and communities express in appropiate ways
locally the degree of communion that already exists"* [44].

Concrete Results

The initiatives undertaken by Faith and Order have contributed
to a growing convergence with respect to numerous other intrinsic
questions of the faith, which are, of course, inextricably bound up
with the ecclesiological debate. One of the most striking examples
in this regard is the rapprochement between the Eastern Orthodox
Churches and the Oriental Orthodox Churches on the interpretation of the christological dogma declared by the Council of Chalcedon in 451 (one person in two natures, which are united uncon-
fusedly, unchangeably, indivisibly and inseparably). What is at
issue here is the old controversy about the relation between the
human and divine natures in Christ, the debate between the so-
called mono- and duophysitists. Basing their case on the well-
known phrase used by Cyril of Alexandria on "the one physis (or
hypothasis) of God's Word Incarnate", representatives of both
church traditions declared that, on the essence of the Christological dogma, they found themselves "in full agreement". During

---

[44] See for the text of this statement on "The Unity of the Church as Koinonia:
Gift and Calling", G. Gassmann (ed.), *Documentary History*, 3-5, esp. 4/5.

four conferences in Aarhus (1964), Bristol (1967), Geneva (1970) and Addis Ababa (1971), there was not only a recognition of the moments of truth in non-extreme forms of mono- and duo-physitism, but also an agreement to explicitly remove the mutual anathemas. In the "Agreed Statement" of Aarhus it was declared:

> *"Since we agree in rejecting without reservation the teaching of Eutyches as well as of Nestorius, the acceptance or non-acceptance of the Council of Chalcedon does not entail the acceptance of either heresy. Both sides found themselves fundamentally following the Christological teaching of the one undivided Church as expressed by St. Cyril".*

In the "Agreed Statement" of Bristol this convergence is subsequently specified in the following formulations:

> *"Ever since the fifth century, we have used different formulae to confess our common faith in the One Lord Jesus Christ, perfect God and perfect Man. Some of us affirm two natures, wills and energies hypostatically united in the One Lord Jesus Christ. Some of us affirm one united divine-human nature, will and energy in the same Christ. But both sides speak of a union without confusion, without change, without division, without separation. The four adverbs belong to our common tradition. Both affirm the dynamic permanence of the Godhead and the Manhood, with all their natural properties and faculties in the one Christ. Those who speak in terms of 'two' do not thereby divide or separate. Those who speak in terms of 'one' do not thereby commingle or confuse".*

In Geneva this agreement was supplemented by the following declaration:

> *"The human will and energy of Christ are neither absorbed nor suppressed by His divine will and energy, nor are the former opposed to the latter, but are united together in perfect concord without division or confusion; He who wills and acts is always the One hypostasis of the Logos Incarnate. One is Emmanuel, God and Man, Our Lord and Saviour, Whom we adore and worship and who yet is one of us"* [45].

---

[45] Cf. P. Gregorios/W.H. Lazareth/N.A. Nissiotis (eds.), *Does Chalcedon Divide or Unite? Towards Convergence in Orthodox Christology*, Geneva 1981, 3, 5/6 and 8 respectively.

The fruits of these unofficial consultations were reaped by the official Joint Commission for Theological Dialogue Between the Orthodox Church and Oriental Orthodox Churches in their agreed statement at the Amba Bishoi Monastery in Wadi-el Natrun (Egypt), 20-24 June 1989. There they even extended their agreement as follows:

> *"Our mutual agreement is not limited to christology, but encompasses the whole faith of the one undivided Church of the early centuries. We are agreed also in our understanding of the Person and work of God the Holy Spirit, who proceeds from the Father alone, and is always adored with the Father and the Son"*[46].

This last sentence is already an allusion to a comparable consensus with no less far-reaching consequences. This consensus took place in the field of the full acknowledgment of each other's being church, between the Eastern and Western churches, with respect to the so-called 'filioque'. What is at issue here is the tendency, which grew ever stronger in the West from the fifth century onwards, to add to the text of the Nicene-Constantinopolitan Creed (381) that the Spirit of God has not proceeded from the Father alone, but also from the Son (filioque).

This development was also officially sanctioned in the declaration of Pope Benedict VIII that the filioque had to be added to the

---

[46] See for the text of the agreement, *Sobornost* 12 (1990) 78-80. Cf. for a short historical introduction to this agreement and for the recommendations of the Joint Commission, H. Meyer/D. Papandreou/H.J. Urban/L. Vischer (Hrsg.), *Dokumente wachsender Übereinstimmung: Sämtliche Berichte und Konsenstexte interkonfessioneller Gespräche auf Weltebene*, Bd.II: 1982-1990, Paderborn-Frankfurt 1992, 294-306. The German text of the above quoted last sentence is less cryptic than the English version: "In unserem Gottesverständnis – Person und Handeln Gottes miteingeschlossen – und in unserem Verständnis des Heiligen Geistes, der allein aus dem Vater hervorgeht und stets zugleich mit dem Vater und dem Sohn verherrlicht wird, stimmen wir ebenfalls überein" (301). This translation is more in agreement with the French original: "Nous sommes d'accord également sur la façon de comprendre la Personne et l'Action de Dieu, le Saint-Esprit qui procède du Père seul, et est toujours adoré avec le Père et le Fils". Cf. "Commission mixte de dialogue entre l'Église orthodoxe et les Églises orientales orthodoxes", *Istina* 34 (1990) 225-230, esp. 228-230 and the instructive article of B. Dupuy, "La 'déclaration approuvée' d'Anba Bichoï (24 juin 1989)", *Istina* 34 (1990) 137-146.

text of this creed for use in the Roman mass. The theological question at issue here is that of the role of the Father as source of the trinity (fons trinitatis) and the role of the Son with regard to the procession of the Spirit.

In the so-called Klingenthal Memorandum (1979), representatives of the Eastern and Western church declare that the Father alone is the principle and cause of the trinity, but that the begetting of the Son from the Father qualifies the procession of the Spirit as a procession from "the Father of the Son". Thereby the intention of the Western filioque has been honoured: the Holy Spirit is none other than the Spirit of Jesus Christ. However, Eastern criticism of the filioque has also been taken into account: the Holy Spirit cannot be subordinated to Christ as if he were a mere instrument of power. With a view to preventing an uninhibited charismatic enthusiasm, it is always to be emphasized that the Holy Spirit is the Spirit of Jesus Christ. However, with a view to preventing an authoritarian institutionalism in which the Holy Spirit is reduced to a possession and instrument in the hands of the earthly representatives of Christ, the specific trinitarian character of the Spirit with regard to Christ is also to be emphasized. This specific trinitarian character is emphasized by the Klingenthal Memorandum in a succinct reference to the biblical covenants in which the Spirit of God is mentioned in communion and in contradistinction to Jesus' life and work:

> "While one might be inclined to connect the coming of the Spirit
> exclusively with Pentecost, it must be remembered that any such
> limitation tends towards Marcionitism in its patent neglect of the
> Old Testament witness to the presence and activity of the Spirit of
> Israel. Moreover, the Spirit is confessed to have been instrumental
> in the coming of Christ ("conceived by the Holy Spirit"), and to
> have been the life-giving power of God in his resurrection. Jesus
> during his ministry promised the sending of the Spirit, and the earliest Christians understood the pouring out of the Spirit at Pentecost to be the fulfilment of that promise. The Spirit **precedes** the
> coming of Jesus, is active **throughout** his life, death and resurrection, and is **also sent** as the Paraclete by Jesus to the believers,

> *who by this sending and receiving are constituted the Church. This*
> *chain of observations suggest that it would be insufficient and*
> *indeed illegitimate to 'read back' into the Trinity only those New*
> *Testament passages which refer to the sending of the Spirit by*
> *Jesus Christ"* [47].

In addition to this far-reaching form of consensus about the pronouncements of the Council of Chalcedon and about the filioque,
the Lima text in particular has been one of the main ecumenical
milestones of the past decades. In the meantime, the text has
already been translated into more than thirty languages and the
'Geneva edition' has already gone through more than 24 reprints.
One may rightly speak of an ecumenical bestseller here[48]. The
three statements on baptism, eucharist and ministry are the fruits
of a 50-year process of study reaching back to the first Faith and
Order Conference at Lausanne in 1927. The material was discussed and revised by the Faith and Order Commission at Accra
(1974), Bangalore (1978) and Lima (1982). Especially from Sep-
tember 1979 onwards, a steering group has worked on the drafting
under the presidency of Frère Max Thurian of the Taizé Community in France. After the final text had been agreed upon at the
Faith and Order Meeting in Lima in 1982, this 'Lima text' was
officially adopted by the Sixth World Assembly of the World
Council of Churches at Vancouver in 1983 and then sent to the

---

[47] See for the text of the Klingenthal Memorandum on "The Filioque Clause in
Ecumenical Perspective", G. Gassmann (ed.), *Documentary History*, 178-190,
esp. 182/183. Cf. also L. Vischer (ed.), *Spirit of God, Spirit of Christ: Ecumeni-*
cal Reflections on the Filioque Controversy (Faith and Order Paper No. 103) Lon-
don-Geneva 1981 with reactions from the various Christian traditions (Anglican,
Old Catholic, Reformed, Eastern-Orthodox and Roman Catholic) to this Memorandum. See further A. Heron, "The Filioque Clause: Questions Raised by Member Churches – Attempt at an Answer", *Reformed World* 39 (1987) 842-852; J.C.
Bauerschmidt, "'Filioque and the Episcopal Church", *Anglican Theological*
Review 73 (1991) 7-25; Th.F. Torrance, "The Doctrine of the Holy Trinity
according to St. Athanasius", *Anglican Theological Review* 71 (1989) 395-405
and Th. Stylianopoulos, "An Ecumenical Solution to the Filioque Question?",
Journal of Ecumenical Studies 28 (1991) 260-280.
[48] *Baptism, Eucharist and Ministry* (Faith and Order Paper No. 111), Geneva
1982.

member churches along with the request for their official response. The latter was a vital step in the ecumenical process of reception. We shall enter at length into the content of the Lima text in chapters IV, V and VI.

Among the concrete results of the work of Faith and Order mention must be made of the longterm work on the 'ecumenical explanation of the Apostolic Faith as it is Confessed in the Nicene-Constantinopolitan Creed (381)'. Unfortunately, there was no process of reception organized around this text in the fashion of the Lima text. Nevertheless, this common explication of the classical doctrine of the trinity may certainly also be reckoned among the ecumenical milestones. Its significance lies mainly in the fact that, after many years of reflection on ecclesiological and sacramental-theological questions, there is now also an explicit concern with the essence of the common Christian faith, the doctrine of the Trinity. It is also clear that this ecclesiological explication has involved the incorporation of a number of insights from modern exegetic and dogma-historical research.

Moreover, it appears from this text, even more strongly than in the Lima text, that the work of Faith and Order still has a strongly Western and Eastern character and that the voice of the church of the southern hemisphere – which now constitutes the majority of Christianity! – is still not distinctly heard. No doubt this is partly due to the strongly historical orientation of this explication as a result of which the answers to modern challenges often turn out to be very scanty indeed. The "Giving Account of the Hope within us" programme was characterized by a most active participation from the side of the southern hemisphere. The fact that there has been no real success in integrating this programme, initiated during the Louvain meeting of Faith and Order in 1971, into the explication of the confession of faith appears, in retrospect, to confirm the Western character of this explication. We shall consider the questions raised here at greater length in chapter III.

All these concrete results of Faith and Order were to a great degree stimulated by the concepts of unity discussed earlier in this chapter. Apart from this, however, they are supported, as to their content, by the often very surprising discovery of the continuous and dynamic interaction between scripture and tradition. This discovery crystallized especially in the sixties, in clear formulations about the relation between the two during both Vatican II (1962-1965) and the Fourth World Conference of Faith and Order at Montreal (Canada) in 1963. We shall, therefore, begin our discussion of 50 years of ecumenical reflection with the striking developments that occurred during these years both on the Protestant and on the Roman Catholic side in the field of the hermeneutics of Bible and tradition.

CHAPTER II

SCRIPTURE AND TRADITION

The Relevance of the Hermeneutical Problem

The relation between Bible and tradition seems at first sight a typically sixteenth century Western problem of the theology of controversy. It seems far removed from our present concern to make the Bible relevant to the great questions of hunger and poverty in the greater part of the world, and to the problems of boredom and meaninglessness in the 'old' Europe and in North America. It cannot be denied: there is, indeed, a large gap between this old book and the present 'book of life'. Nevertheless, believers still derive hope and expectation from this 'old' book which, in their opinion, is still life-renewing today. Therefore, the present-day outlook on life, and the orientation of the witness of Israel and the New Testament community to the one God of life do not have to be regarded in opposition to one another. To be sure, the connecting link is the God of all centuries who also addresses His message to us.

These two ideas, namely, that the Bible is the book which deals with the God of all life, and that it is a witness addressed to us, time and again encourage believers to try and bridge the gap between that word from "the highest heaven" (Luke 2:14) and our humble position (Luke 1:46-55). In a theological sense, then, we speak of a hermeneutic problem in reference to Hermes, the messenger of the gods in Greek mythology. It was Hermes' task to explain to humans the decisions and plans of their gods. Thus, he bridged the gap between the divine and the human realm. Similarly, hermeneutics is concerned with examining the relationship between two realms, the realm of the text on the one hand, and the people who wish to understand it on the other hand[1].

Assuming that we know where the story about our 'humble position' is to be found – in the hymn of Mary, which nowadays means: in the street, in the newspapers and on television – the next most weighty question is: where is the high word of God to be found and who is to explain it to us: Who can us give the clue? (Acts 8,31).

This question of the Ethiopian on his way home from Jerusalem is our question as well. Theologically formulated, it is the question of where God's revelation is to be found and the question of the authoritative explication. Thus, in the complex of questions around the relationship between Scripture and tradition it is always a matter of two central questions. One question concerns the relationship between God and humanity: how can people understand a divine word? The other question concerns the relationship between human beings: how can people understand each other throughout the centuries and in different contexts. These two central hermeneutical questions, therefore, have both a vertical and a horizontal dimension.

With these two questions at the back of our minds, we shall first concentrate on a number of classical texts from the Council of Trent and from the time of the Reformation. Our aim is to consider how much of these stands was preserved during the Second Vatican Council and at the Fourth World Conference on Faith and Order at Montreal in 1963, and to reflect on the shift of accents. Then, we shall try to illustrate the shifts of positions by means of the reactions of the member churches of the World Council of Churches to the Lima text, as they have now been summarized in an evaluative report. Finally, we conclude the treatment of this theme with a reference to a pronouncement of the Fifth World Conference of Faith and Order at Santiago de Compostela in 1993 on the tension between unity and diversity within the canon.

[1] Cf. for example W.G. Jeanrond, *Theological Hermeneutics: Development and Significance*, London (1991) 1994, 1.

The Historical Problem

In opposition to the Reformers, the Council of Trent, in its fourth session of 1546, the first which was really about content, immediately took a clear stand with respect to the sounds heard from the churches of the Reformation:

> "The holy, ecumenical, and general Council of Trent, ... has always as its purpose to remove error and preserve in the Church the purity of the gospel that was originally promised by the prophets in Sacred Scripture and first promulgated by the Son of God himself, our Lord Jesus Christ. He, in turn, ordered his apostles, who are the source of all saving truth and moral teaching, to preach it to every creature (see Matt. 28:19f.; Mark 16:15). The council is aware that this truth and teaching are contained in written books and in the unwritten traditions (in libris scriptis, et sine scripto traditionibus) that the apostles received from Christ himself or that were handed on, as it were from hand to hand, from the apostles under the inspiration of the Holy Spirit, and so have come down to us. The council follows the example of the orthodox Fathers and with the same sense of devotion and reverence (pari pietatis affectu, ac reverentia) with which it accepts and venerates all the books both of the Old and the New Testament, since one God is the author of both, it also accepts and venerates traditions concerned with faith and morals as having been received orally from Christ or inspired by the Holy Spirit and continuously preserved in the Catholic Church" [2].

The Council declares here that "the purity of the gospel" was transmitted both in writing and orally, either literally from the lips of Christ, or inspired – the Latin text even says dictated – by the Holy Spirit. Regarding the question of the authoritative explication, this same Council observes:

> "Furthermore, to keep undisciplined minds under proper control, the council decrees that no one should dare to rely on his own judgment in matters of faith and morals affecting the structure of

---

[2] Cf. *The Church Teaches: Documents of the Church in English Translation*, Rockford 1973, 44/45; Latin: H. Denzinger/A. Schönmetzer (eds.), *Enchiridion Symbolorum Definitionum et Declarationum de rebus fidei et morum*, Barcinone-Friburgi Brisgoviae-Romae 1976[36], 364/365 (No. 783/1501).

> *Christian doctrine and to distort Sacred Scripture to fit meanings*
> *of his own that are contrary to the meaning that the holy mother*
> *Church has held and now holds; for it is its office to judge about*
> *the true sense and interpretation of Sacred Scripture. Nor should*
> *anyone dare to interpret Sacred Scripture contrary to the unani-*
> *mous agreement of the Fathers, even though such interpretations*
> *are never going to be published"* [3].

The voice from the Reformation cannot be reproduced con-
cisely by means of conciliar texts, since the Reformation does not
know any central doctrinal authority. A certain authority, however,
may be assigned to confessional texts confirmed by synods. As far
as the Calvinist tradition is concerned, the Second Helvetic Confession of 1566 is the most explicit. Regarding Sacred Scripture
this confession says:

> *"We believe and confess the canonical Scriptures of the holy*
> *prophets and apostles of both Testaments to be the true Word of*
> *God, and to have sufficient authority of themselves, not of men.*
> *For God himself spoke to the fathers, prophets, apostles, and still*
> *speaks to us through the Holy Scriptures.*
> *And in this Holy Scripture, the universal Church of Christ has the*
> *most complete exposition of all that pertains to a saving faith, and*
> *also to the framing of a life acceptable to God; and in this respect*
> *it is expressly commanded by God that nothing be either added to*
> *or taken from the same".*

And with regard to the true interpretation of Scripture it is
observed:

> *"The apostle Peter has said that the Holy Scriptures are not of*
> *private interpretation (II Peter 1:20), and thus we do not allow all*
> *possible interpretations. .... We hold that interpretation to be*
> *orthodox and genuine which is gleaned from the Scriptures them-*
> *selves ... and which agree with the rule of faith and love, and con-*
> *tributes much to the glory of God and man's salvation"* [4].

---

[3] *The Church Teaches*, 46; Latin: *Enchiridion*, 366 (No. 786/1507).
[4] See for the English Text, *The Book of Confessions: Part I of the Constitution of
the United Presbyterian Church in the United State of America*, New York 1970[2],
5.001 and 5.010. Latin: Ph. Schaff (ed.), *Creeds of Christendom*, Vol.III: Evangelical Creeds, Grand Rapids 1966, 233-306, esp. 237 and 239.

In spite of this clear choice of the hermeneutic maxim, 'sacra scriptura sui ipsius interpres', ecclesial and ministerial concerns continued to play a role in Protestant exegesis. This is reflected in Heinrich Heppe's standard work on *Reformed Dogmatics*, in which he first reproduces the above-mentioned hermeneutic principle, while referring to the famous *Leiden Synopsis* (1581), a summary of Reformed theology, composed by the professors of the faculty of theology of the University of Leiden (The Netherlands):

> *"The most penetrating discussion of the question, 'who is the lawful interpreter of H. Scripture?' is to be found in the Leiden Synopsis (Disp.V). It says first of all: 'In order that this question may be correctly explained according to the norm of God's Word, we say that Scripture is its own interpreter, or rather God, speaking in the Scriptures and through the Scriptures. In the clearer and essential passages He openly indicates His will to believers, as was previously shown. In obscure passages He more and more confirms the same will of His for them by comparison of them with clearer passages".*

However, – again quoting the *Leiden Synopsis* – Heppe goes on to observe that since God avails Himself of the ministry of men, it must be acknowledged:

> *"that in Christ's true Church there is also another class of interpreters, the ministerial, constituted under both God and His Word, to which also in H. Scripture the power of judging is assigned"* [5].

In the Lutheran confessional writings, too, a church element also plays a part in determining the explication of Scripture, even though one is most explicit as to what one thinks of the appeal to church "traditions": they are *traditiones humanae institutae*, instituted by man [6].

---

[5] Cf. H. Heppe, *Reformed Dogmatics: Set out and illustrated from the Sources*, Grand Rapids 1978, 35. Heppe refers here to the *Synopsis purioris Theologiae*, Leiden 1581 (1652[6]), Disp.V, 27. In support of the recognition of the necessity of ministerial interpretation the *Synopsis* refers to a great many scriptural passages: 2 Chron.19:8; Ezek.44:24; Zech.3:7; I Cor.2:15; I Cor.10:15 and I Cor.14:29.
[6] Cf. *The Augsburg Confession* (1530), pars I,XV and pars II, V in the edition of Ph. Schaff (ed.), *Creeds of Christendom*, Vol.III, 16 and 42.

In opposition to this, it is asserted that:

> *"We believe, teach, and confess that the prophetic and apostolic writings of the Old and New Testaments are the only rule and norm according to which all doctrines and teachers alike must be appraised and judged"* [7].

However, in Edmund Schlink's summary of the Reformation position to which Lutherans are committed, a church element does indeed appear to play a part when he stresses the summary character of the confessions. His argumentation is fourfold:

1. The sole norm of all teaching in the church is the Holy Scripture of the Old and New Testaments. Church Fathers are cited in the Book of Concord, but neither they nor statements from church history nor reason are allowed as norm for doctrine.

2. Holy Scripture is the norm because it is the prophetic and apostolic witness to the Gospel. The Gospel is the norm in Scripture and Scripture is the norm for the sake of the Gospel.

3. Confessions, such as those in the Book of Concord, are an exposition and summary of Scripture, a witness to the Gospel; they are further a gift of the Spirit.

4. The Confession is exposition of Scripture in consensus with the church of past centuries, in the face of current needs and heresies[8].

Vatican II and Montreal

Some four centuries later, during Vatican II (1962-1965) and the Fourth World Conference of Faith and Order, we clearly see positions starting to move, although the continuity with the past of the church – including the literal formulations – is also quite

---

[7] Cf. the *Formula of Concord*, Epitome I in: Th.G. Tappert (ed.), *The Book of Concord: The Confessions of the Evangelical Lutheran Church*, Philadelphia 1959, 464.

[8] See E. Schlink, *Theology of the Lutheran Confessions*, Philadelphia 1961, 1-22. Cf. further J. Reumann/J.A. Fitzmyer, "Scripture as Norm for our Common Faith", *Midstream* 30 (1993) 81-107.

explicitly preserved. This appears very clearly from the Dogmatic Constitution on Divine Revelation, *Dei Verbum*, No.9 where the Council declares:

> "*Sacred Tradition and sacred Scripture ... are bound closely together, and communicate one with the other. For both of them, flowing out from the same divine well-spring, come together in some fashion to form one thing, and move towards the same goal. Sacred Scripture is the speech of God as it is put down in writing under the breath of the Holy Spirit. And Tradition transmits in its entirety the Word of God which has been entrusted to the apostles by Christ the Lord and the Holy Spirit. It transmits it to the successors of the apostles so that, enlightened by the Spirit of truth, they may faithfully preserve, expound and spread it abroad by their preaching. Thus it comes about that the Church does not draw her certainty about all revealed truths from the holy Scriptures alone. Hence, both Scripture and Tradition must be accepted and honored with equal feelings of devotion and reverence (pari pietatis affectu ac reverentia)*".

With respect to the authentic interpretation of Scripture the tenth paragraph observes that:

> "*But the task of giving an authentic interpretation of the Word of God, whether in its written form or in the form of Tradition, has been entrusted to the living teaching office of the Church alone. Its authority in this matter is exercised in the name of Jesus Christ. Yet this Magisterium is not superior to the Word of God, but is its servant. It teaches only what has been handed on to it. At the divine command and with the help of the Holy Spirit, it listens to this devotedly, guards it with dedication and expounds it faithfully. All that it proposes for belief as being divinely revealed is drawn from this single deposit of faith.*
> *It is clear, therefore, that, in the supremely wise arrangement of God, sacred Tradition, sacred Scripture and the Magisterium of the Church are so connected and associated that one of them cannot stand without the others. Working together, each in its own way under the action of the one Holy Spirit, they all contribute effectively to the salvation of souls*".

When the Faith and Order World Conference met at the (Roman Catholic) Mc Gill University in July, 1963, the definite text of *Verbum Dei* was not yet available. An early draft, *De Fontibus*, had

been withdrawn after it had run into vehement opposition at the first
session of the Council, in November, 1962. In July, 1963, the first
draft of a new text was still on the drawing board. It would be dis-
tributed to the bishops during the second session of Vatican II, in
September-November of 1963[9]. Especially via a number of Roman
Catholic observers, there was rather direct contact with what was
going on in Rome. Another important factor in Montreal was the
presence of a large delegation from Eastern-Orthodoxy which, since
the Third World Assembly of the World Council of Churches at
New Delhi in 1961, has been considerably more amply represented
within the World Council than before. Both church influences in
Montreal, combined with the digestion of a number of important
developments from the field of New Testament scholarship, brought
about an ecumenical breakthrough in the stereotypical thinking of
the theology of controversy about Scripture and tradition.

From the Tridentine pronouncements, it may already be inferred
that it is in fact impossible to speak of "two sources". In the
decade of the 1950's, a number of historical and theological studies examined the decree of the fourth session of the Council of
Trent (1546), which dealt with 'the reception of the sacred books
and the traditions'. This historical research and the accompanying
theological reflection oriented the interpretation of the Tridentine
decree away from the point of view of the nineteenth century,
when it was commonly taught that Scripture and tradition constitute two distinct sources of faith. According to the interpretations
of Tavard, Geiselmann and Congar[10] there is one single source

[9] Cf. G.H. Tavard, "The Ecumenical Search for Tradition: Thirty Years after the
Montreal Statement", *Journal of Ecumenical Studies* 30 (1993) 315-329, esp. 316.
See further Idem (ed.), *Dogmatic Constitution of Divine Revelation of Vatican
Council II: Commentary and Translation*, Glen Rock 1966.
[10] Cf. G.H. Tavard, *Holy Writ or Holy Church: The Crisis of the Protestant
Reformation*, New York 1959; J.R. Geiselmann, "Das Konzil von Trient über das
Verhältnis der Heiligen Schrift und der nichtgeschriebenen Traditionen" in: M.
Schmaus (ed.), *Die mündliche Überlieferung*, München 1957 and Y. Congar, *La
Tradition et les traditions*, Vol.I: Essai Historique, Paris 1960 and Vol.II: Essai
Théologique, Paris 1963. This last volume, finished in Januari 1963, has been
dedicated to both the members of the Faith and Order Commissions on Tradition
and those of Vatican II. See for a succinct summary of the different interpretations

which is handed down to us in two ways: in writing via the Scriptures and orally via the bishops as successors of the apostles. Vatican II, in *Dei Verbum*, No.7, 8 and 10, expresses itself very clearly on the sufficiency (sufficientia) of this single source:

> *"This Gospel was to be the source of all saving truth and moral discipline" (7); "What was handed on by the apostles comprises everything that serves to make the People of God live their lives in holiness and increase their faith" (8) and "Sacred Tradition and sacred Scripture make up a single sacred deposit of the Word of God, which is entrusted to the Church" (10).*

While Vatican II does indeed assume a close interdependence of Scripture and tradition, because of their roots in the one source, it nevertheless goes on speaking about two separate entities:

> *"This sacred Tradition, then, and the sacred Scripture of both Testaments, are like a mirror, in which the Church, during its pilgrim journey here on earth, contemplates God, from whom the Church receives everything" (7).*

In this respect, Montreal, especially because of the discovery in New Testament research that the Bible itself is already the reflection of many traditions, goes one step further. Now we see that the concept of Tradition (with a capital T) is interpreted in such a way that it may comprise the other two concepts, Scripture and tradition(s). The concept of Tradition now represents the one source:

> *"We speak of the **Tradition** (with a capital T), **tradition** (with a small t) and **traditions**. By the **Tradition** is meant the Gospel itself, transmitted from generation to generation in and by the Church, Christ himself present in the life of the Church. By **tradition** is meant the traditionary process. The term **traditions** is used in two senses, to indicate both the diversity of forms of expression and also what we call confessional traditions, for instance the Lutheran or the Reformed tradition. In the latter part of our report the word appears in a further sense, when we speak of cultural traditions" (II,39)*[11].

J. Beumer, *Die mündliche Überlieferung als Glaubensquelle* (Handbuch der Dogmengeschichte, Bd.I, Fasz.4), Freiburg-Basel-Wien, 1962, 74-88 ("Das Konzil von Trient").
[11] Cf. G. Gassmann (ed.), *Documentary History*, 10.

As far as this attempt at a conceptual definition is concerned, it is important not to complicate matters by overemphasizing the distinction between tradition (singular) and traditions (plural). The distinction between the threefold use of the concept of tradition, namely as Tradition, tradition and traditions takes its origin from the report of the North American section, where it means that, in explanation of the origin of the various church traditions, reference is made to the phenomenon of transmission necessary for interhuman intercourse. For this transmission process or communication process one employs the word tradition in singular[12].

During the Montreal conference, however, this concept of transmission was both incorporated in the definition of Tradition with a capital T "as paradosis of the Gospel", and in the definition of the "dynamic transmission of the Tradition" in the history of the various church traditions. The process of transmission is the pre-supposition of both the concept of Tradition and of the various church traditions. With a view to typifying this process, and in order to prevent unnecessary complications, it is better to speak of transmission and paradosis and then concentrate on the scope of this speech about Tradition and traditions.

In Montreal the issue at stake was the grateful acknowledgement, on the part of Christians, that God has revealed himself in the history of the people of God in the Old Testament and in Jesus Christ, his Son, the mediator between God and humankind. The testimony of prophets and apostles inaugurated the Tradition of his revelation. The once-for-all disclosure of God in Jesus Christ inspired the apostles and disciples to give witness to the revelation given in the person and work of Christ.

The oral and written tradition of the prophets and apostles, under the guidance of the Holy Spirit, led to the formation of Scriptures and to the canonization of the Old and New Testaments as the Bible of the Church. The very fact that Tradition precedes

---

[12] Cf. for the text of the report of the North American Section, *Report on Tradition and Traditions* (Faith and Order Paper No.40), Geneva 1963, 7-29 ("The Renewal of the Christian Tradition").

the Scriptures points to the significance of tradition, but also to the Bible as the treasure of the Word of God[13]. This line of argumentation of Montreal is exactly the same as that of *Dei Verbum*, No.7 and that of Trent:

> "God graciously arranged that the things he had once revealed for the salvation of all peoples should remain in their entirety, throughout the ages, and be transmitted to all generations. Therefore, Christ the Lord, in whom the entire Revelation of the most high God is summed up (cf. 2 Cor.1:20;3:16-4:6) commanded his apostles to preach the Gospel, which had been promised beforehand by the prophets, and which he fulfilled in his own person and promulgated with his own lips. In preaching the Gospel they were to communicate the gifts of God to all men. This Gospel was to be the source of all saving truth and moral discipline. This was faithfully done: it was done by the apostles who handed on, by the spoken word of their preaching, by the example they gave, by the institutions they established, what they themselves had received – whether from the lips of Christ, from his way of life and his works, or whether they had learned it at the prompting of the Holy Spirit; it was done by those apostles and other men associated with the apostles who, under the inspiration of the same Holy Spirit, committed the message of salvation to writing".

Therefore, our starting point is that we are all living in a tradition which goes back to our Lord and has its roots in the Old Testament, and that we are all indebted to that Tradition inasmuch as we have received the revealed truth, the Gospel, by reason of its being transmitted from one generation to another:

> "Thus we can say that we exist as Christians by the Tradition of the Gospel (the **paradosis** of the **kerygma**) testified in Scripture, transmitted in and by the Church through the power of the Holy Spirit" (II,45)[14].

Tradition, taken in this sense, is actualized in the preaching of the Word, in the administration of the Sacraments and worship, in Christian teaching and theology, and in mission and witness to Christ in the lives of the members of the Church. What is trans-

---

[13] Cf. G. Gassmann (ed.), *Documentary History*, 11.
[14] G. Gassmann (ed.), *Documentary History*, 11.

mitted in the process of tradition is the Christian faith, not only as a sum of tenets, but as a living reality transmitted through the operation of the Holy Spirit. However, this Tradition, which is the work of the Holy Spirit, is embodied in traditions in the two senses of the word, both as referring to diversity in forms of expression, and in the sense of separate communions.

According to the Dutch Reformed theologian, Ellen Flesseman-van Leer, one of the most stimulating figures in the Faith and Order studies on Scripture, the significance of the Montreal report lies in the recognition that Tradition and Scripture are not two independent entities. They are so intertwined that neither, taken by itself, can simply be used as authoritative.

The Reformation principle of *sola scriptura* is qualified by the reminder that the Bible is part of Tradition and embedded in Tradition; in fact, it becomes living Tradition as it is rightly interpreted in ever new situations.

On the other hand, Tradition, as source of revelation, is qualified by the assertion that it is only accessible in traditions whose trustworthiness must be tested in the light of Scripture[15]. On the basis of what has been stated above, it was even proposed, in Montreal, to declare that we exist as Christians *sola traditione*, by tradition alone. However, both Max Thurian of Taizé (France) and Ernst Käsemann of Germany said that, although they accepted the term *sola traditione* in this context, they thought it would certainly be impossible to maintain it for wider use; it would unquestionably cause serious misunderstandings, especially among Protestants already suspious of the WCC and accustomed to *sola Scriptura* as the battle-cry of the Reformation. Nevertheless – as the editors of the conference report optimistically observe – the phrase is perhaps difficult only because it is premature; it is likely, when used as summarizing a whole understanding of Tradition in this sense, to be of real value in ecumenical work. Such a use of it will,

---

[15] Cf. E. Flesseman-van Leer (ed.), *The Bible, its Authority and Interpretation in the Ecumenical Movement* (Faith and Order Paper No 99), Geneva 1980, 3. See also M. Haudel, *Die Bibel und die Einheit der Kirchen: Eine Untersuchung der Studien von 'Glauben und Kirchenverfassung'*, Göttingen 1993.

however, also need to take into account the warning notes sounded in the discussion on behalf of Scripture, if not of *sola Scriptura*. In particular, one can ask: Where is this Tradition to be found authoritatively? In the different traditions?[16]

The Quest for a Hermeneutical Principle

The traditions in Christian history are distinct from, and yet connected with, this Tradition. They are expressions and manifestations, in diverse historical forms, of the one truth and reality which is Christ. However, while these traditions can be faithful transmissions of the Gospel, they can also represent serious distortions of it. In this ambiguity the seriousness of the problem of tradition is indicated. Where do we find the right criterion?

When the canon of the New Testament was finally defined and recognized by the Church, it was still more natural to use this body of writings as a first and indispensable criterion. However, it cannot be the only criterion, because the Tradition in its written form, as Holy Scripture, has to be interpreted by the Church in ever new situations. Such an interpretation of the Tradition is to be found in the crystallization of tradition in the creeds, in the liturgical forms of the sacraments and other forms of worship, and also in the preaching of the Word and in theological expositions of the doctrine of the Church. A mere reiteration of the words of Holy Scripture would be a betrayal of the Gospel which has to be made understandable and has to convey a challenge to the world.

It will be clear that the necessity of interpretation again raises the question of the criterion for the genuine Tradition. Here, we arrive at the quest for a hermeneutical principle. This problem has been dealt with in different ways by the various churches searching for internal and external principles. In some confessional tra-

---

[16] P.C. Rodger/L. Vischer (eds.), *The Fourth World Conference on Faith and Order: The Report from Montreal 1963* (Faith and Order Paper No. 42), London 1964, 24-25.

ditions the accepted internal hermeneutical principle has been that any portion of Scripture is to be interpreted in the light of Scripture as a whole. In others, the hermeneutical principle has been sought in what is considered to be the centre of Holy Scripture. The emphasis here has been primarily on the Incarnation, or on Atonement and Redemption, or on Justification by Faith, or on the message of the nearness of the Kingdom of God, or on the ethical teachings of Jesus. In still others, all emphasis is laid upon what Scripture says to the individual conscience, under the guidance of the Holy Spirit.

In the Orthodox Church, the external hermeneutical principle is found in the mind of the Church, especially as this is expressed in the Fathers of the Church in the Ecumenical Councils. In the Roman Catholic Church, the external principle is found in the deposit of faith, of which the Church's *magisterium* is the guardian. In still other traditions, the creeds, complemented by confessional documents or by the definitions of Ecumenical Councils and the witness of the Fathers, are considered to provide the right principle for the understanding of Scripture. In all of these cases, where the principle of interpretation is found elsewhere than in Scripture, the authority of this (external) principle is not thought to be alien to the central concept of Holy Scripture. On the contrary, it is considered precisely to provide a key to the understanding of what is said in Scripture.

The problem, however, is that loyalty to our confessional understanding of Holy Scripture produces much convergence but remarkably more divergence in the interpretation of Scripture. Therefore, the question arises as to how we can overcome the situation in which we read Scripture only in the light of our own traditions. In this regard it seems important not only to stress the different past of the tradition, but the common future as well.

The Tradition, in its content, not only looks backward to its origin in the past but also forward to the fullness which shall be revealed. The life of the Church is lived in the continuous recalling, appropriation and transmission of the once-for-all event of Christ's coming in the flesh, and in the eager expectation of his coming in glory. All this finds expression in the Word and in the

Sacraments in which "we proclaim the Lord's death till he come" (I Cor. 11:26). This means that the Tradition must be handed on in time and also in space. In other words, Tradition has a vital missionary dimension in every country. Whatever differences of interpretation there may be, all traditions agree that there is this dynamic element in the Tradition.

When the Word became flesh, the Gospel came to man through a particular cultural medium, that of the Palestinian world at the time. Hence, when the Church takes the Tradition to new peoples, it is necessary that the essential content should again find expression in terms of new cultures. Then we will discover this important phenomenon: the traditionary process involves the dialectic, both of relating the Tradition as completely as possible to every separate cultural situation in which people live, and, at the same time, of demonstrating its transcendence of all that divides people from one another. From this comes the truth that the more the Tradition is expressed in the varying terms of particular cultures, the more its universal character will be fully revealed. It is only "with all the saints" that we will come to know the fullness of Christ's love and glory (Eph.3: 18-19).

Continuity and Discontinuity

All teaching of the church must be based on the *memoria* of God's great deeds in history. Radical departure from, or discontinuity with, the apostolic witness is rejected by all churches. But how is this continuity to be understood?

Inevitably, all traditions recognize that, in the course of the centuries, there have been shifts or modifications. There are – according to the Faith and Order report "How does the church teach authoritatively today?" (1977)[17] – at least three different approaches to the relationship between continuity and discontinuity:

---

[17] See for the text of the report, G. Gassmann (ed.), *Documentary History*, 240-255.

a) Some would claim there have been shifts and modifications at a lower level of change in terminology, practice and structures. They posit an original purity and completeness of a deposit of teaching which can be preserved through the ages with minor adjustments.

b) Others recognize that there have been real shifts in teaching, but regard these as harmonious developments or organic growth.

c) Still others maintain that the discontinuity goes further. In order to make the Gospel actual and contemporary, the teaching of the past may need to be recast. They see continuity in the liberating message of the Gospel rather than in the various teachings in which the message has been actualized. Only the demands of the Gospel can determine what must be retained and what must be altered for the sake of faithfulness.

The issue of continuity and discontinuity has been further complicated by the growing awareness of diversity within the apostolic witness itself. Historical critical methods in biblical studies have led to the recognition that the variety of witnesses within the New Testament reaches much further than was assumed by past generations. Ongoing authoritative teaching based on the apostolic witness has become more difficult for the churches which acknowledge the variety of witnesses in the New Testament. Especially for them, the question arises of how the church acquires certainty as to the fact that what is being taught is in authentic agreement with the Gospel? Here, too, the answers of the various traditions differ in their emphases:

a) Some, while not excluding other authorities, emphasize the authority which is inherent in a certain office. If the bearer of that office has spoken, the teaching can be trusted as truth.

b) Other traditions emphasize the role of confessional documents as an important means of safeguarding the authenticity of teaching. Since these documents have been acknowledged by these traditions as being in accordance with the Scriptures, conformity with them can be regarded as a criterion for the authenticity of the teaching.

c) Other traditions have difficulties in accepting as criteria either the authority of an office or confessional documents. In their view, there cannot be any criterion for authenticity outside the consciousness of the whole people of God. Teaching proves its authenticity by being received and appropriated by the people of God, living in conformity with the Gospel, celebrating the eucharist and fulfilling its prophetic and priestly calling in the world.

d) Still others, while not denying the need for an office or the value of confessional statements, insist on the role of every community and every believer in verifying the authenticity of the teaching which is offered.

This complex hermeneutical situation leads to the question: Can the ecumenical movement, by bringing together churches with different ways of verification, lead to a more comprehensive approach? Can churches be strengthened in their witness by the teaching of another church, even if that church has received it as authoritative in a way that differs from their own? Can the churches, by striving to perfect their ongoing teaching within the framework of their tradition but in dialogical relation to each other, move step by step to greater unity and thus reflect more fully the catholicity of the Church?

Developments after Montreal

The responses of the churches to the Lima text are a particularly informative illustration of the discussion concerning Scripture and tradition within Faith and Order. The following provisional considerations can be formulated[18]:

a) Tradition, Scripture and church cannot be treated as separated phenomena. The ecclesial character of the transmission process cannot be denied. There is no Tradition without concrete human

---

[18] Cf. *Baptism, Eucharist & Ministry 1982-1990: Report on the Process and Responses*, Geneva 1990, 131-142.

traditions, there is no Scripture without a community of believers and there is no church without the God-given Tradition or without the living word of God in the Scriptures.

b) The whole process of transmission comes under the criterion of faithful witness to the gospel, preached by the apostles, of God's free grace and truth.

c) Thus this Tradition is not limited to fixed texts, like Scriptures or the creeds or the sacramental forms of the early church, but also implies the living word of God, Christ incarnate, and the life-giving Spirit, who lead the church into the truth. This Tradition means a permanent dialogue of the church with Christ, an unbroken communion with the divine life, a permanent presence of the Holy Spirit.

d) The post-apostolic tradition in its diverse forms of teaching with regard to faith and practices of life and worship, is always obliged to be a faithful reflection of the apostolic truth of the Tradition. It is interpretative and receptive, based on apostolic faith as its source.

e) The Scriptures, as a unique, divine gift of grace to the people of God, are themselves both the fruit of the prophetic and apostolic tradition and the seed and impulse of the ongoing process of transmission and reception. This process is seen as a continuing, future-oriented and indeed eschatological, dynamic and living event (cf. I Cor.13:12: "Now we see but a poor reflection; then we shall see face to face. Now I know in part; then I shall know fully, even as I am fully known").

f) The ecumenical dialogue itself can be seen as a unique opportunity in which the hermeneutical process takes place under the commonly acknowledged authority of God's word. The paradosis of the gospel is received within a continuous re-reading, reception and reappropriation of the narrative of God's salvation.

g) Tradition (*paradosis*) and communion (*koinonia*) presuppose each other. They intend both past and present: there is a need to discern a continuity of the apostolic faith and of the believing community in history. However, there also has to be a contemporary solidarity of local churches united in faith and reconciled in a universal communion[19].

The many tensions which, however, still continue to exist, were quite manifest at the Fifth World Conference on Faith and Order in Santiago de Compostela (1993). Here, on the one hand, there is an emphatic insistence that the canon creates unity. Moreover, a certain part of the doctrinal tradition of the Church, namely, the Nicene-Constantinopolitan Creed, is explicitly posited as a continuation of the canon. It is declared that this creed, too, created unity. On the other hand, there is also an awareness of the fact that the canon itself is quite diverse and that, therefore, a diversity of interpretations of that canon is legitimate. On the basic of this second approach, it is possible to arrive at a concept of catholicity which is assumed to comprise the whole of the various biblical witnesses:

> "The canon of Scripture grounds the God-given unity of the Church especially in the truth of the Gospel (Gal.2:5 and 14) and teachings which where later set forth and extended in the Nicene-Constantinopolitan Creed. To deny this unity and these teachings is to place oneself outside Christianity. The canon of Scripture also grounds diversity in the Church, not only because of variety in Scripture and the various situations in which Scripture was written, but also because of variety in approaches and interpretations (there is a long history of finding multiple meanings in a passage), and in one's standpoint or that of the community. Churches need to make clear their criteriological principles for the interpretation of Scripture (e.g. tradition, liturgical-sacramental context, justification by faith, experience, etc.). Because the one canon of Scripture exhibits such a wealth of theological diversity, it challenges the churches to grow in catholicity by assimilating the totality of the biblical witness" [20].

In view of the inclusion of a certain part of the doctrinal tradition in this concept of unity all the questions concerning the unity

---

[19] Cf. for these six main points in the ecumenenical dicussion on scripture and tradition *Baptism, Eucharist & Ministry 1982-1990*, 137-140.
[20] *Fifth World Conference on Faith and Order*, 17/18 and Th.F. Best/G. Gassmann (eds.), *On the way to Fuller Koinonia*, 241.

of the canon are also immediately related to all the questions concerning the unity of the doctrinal tradition. However, as the debate on that unity makes clear, the above-mentioned reference to the Nicene-Constantinopolitan Creed is less self-evident than was suggested in Santiago. The matter of that debate will be considered in the following chapter.

CHAPTER III

CONFESSING THE ONE FAITH

Louvain 1971

Whenever Christians put to themselves the question of their common confession of faith, there are always two fundamental options: the first takes its lead from the conviction that 'we are not the first' and thinks in terms of conformity to that cloud of witnesses who went before us; the second takes its lead from the voice of contemporary witnesses around us and involves listening to present-day, contemporary, weeping Rachels, complaining Jobs, fearless Samuels, sagacious Marys and plodding Marthas[1].

When the Fifth World Assembly of the World Council of Churches at Nairobi in 1975 put the common expression of the apostolic faith on the ecumenical agenda, there was hardly any awareness of the acrimony of this dilemma. With no apparent bias, it was declared that:

> *"We ask the churches to undertake a common effort to receive, reappropriate and confess together, as contemporary occasion requires, the Christian truth and faith, delivered through the apostles and handed down through the centuries. Such common action, arising from free and inclusive discussion under the commonly acknowledged authority of God's word, must aim both to clarify and to embody the unity and the diversity which are proper to the church's life and mission"[2].*

---

[1] See on these two possible ways, L. Vischer, "Confessio Fidei in der ökumenischen Diskussion" in: G.J. Békés/H. Meyer (eds.), *Confessio Fidei: International Colloquium Rome, 3-8 November 1980* (Studia Anselminiana 81 – Sacramentum 7), Roma 1982, 17-36, esp. 17-20. Cf. also Idem, "An Ecumenical Creed? An Attempt at a Synthesis", *Concilium* 118 (1978) No. 8 (special issue: "An Ecumenical Confession of Faith?"), 103-118.

[2] G. Gassmann (ed.), *Documentary History*, 30.

However, four years earlier, the Louvain Faith and Order conference (1971) had already conceived the common expression of
our faith quite explicitly as part of the project, "Giving Account of
the Hope that is in us", a project which was strongly contextual in
character[3]. The tenor at the time at Louvain was quite expressly
the idea that "the common expression of our faith" can only be
adequately formulated in one way, namely "by giving account of
the hope within us". Hence, the goal of the study project is explicitly described as: giving account of our hope, instead of formulating a confession.

From the impressive, sometimes even heart-rending testimonies
collected from many continents within the framework of this project, it is patently obvious how concretely and consequently con-
textually this contemporary witness was interpreted[4]. However,

[3] Allan Falconer, the successor of Günther Gassmann as director of Faith and
Order, in his historical retrospective of the work of Faith and Order observes
about this project: "This study invited churches, individuals and groups to share
with each other their contemporary confession of faith. From this process it
became clear that another [alongside Scripture and tradition] distinctive factor
affecting the interpretation of the gospel is the cultural context in which the faith
is being confessed". Cf. A. Falconer, "En Route to Santiago: The Work of the
Faith and Order Commission from Montreal 1963 to Santiago de Compostela
1993", *The Ecumenical Review* 45 (1993) 44-54, esp. 46.
[4] Cf. for the intention of this study project, *Faith and Order Louvain 1971:
Study Reports and Documents* (Faith and Order Paper, No. 59), Geneva 1971,
215/216 and 239/240 where it is observed with respect to the study project,
Giving Account: "At this preliminary stage our suggestion is that individual
groups reflect on and bring to expression what they understand as the salvation
of God, for which they give thanks in worship, and which they are commissioned
to proclaim. The task should be approached by groups in various situations, consisting both of members of different Churches, and of members of the same confessional families"(215). Under the heading of "Conspectus of Studies to be carried out", the project "Common Expression of Faith" is first mentioned. This is
given the sub-title of "Giving account of the hope that is in us; cf. I Peter 3:15"
(239). About the purpose of this study project it is said: "The study will not aim
at the formulation of a creed or confession; it will rather be an effort to give
account of our faith today" (239). Cf. for the result of this study project the
many, often very impressive witnesses of hope from the various continents in the
volumes edited by the Taiwanese Choan-Seng Song *Giving Account of the Hope
Today* (Faith and Order Paper No. 81), Geneva 1976 and *Giving Account of the
Hope Together* (Faith and Order Paper No. 86), Geneva 1978. See also the
reports of the Faith and Order Meetings at Accra and Bangalore, resp. *Uniting in*

this approach also makes patently obvious that it is not at all easy to trace what is common in the midst of the multitude of witnesses, not even when these witnesses assume the slightly more crystallized form of creeds[5].

That is why it does not take long for a countermovement to commence within the World Council of Churches which, looking back historically, bases itself on a so-called 'building period' of the church. Here, one starts from the presupposition that over against the extremely variegated character of the contemporary witnesses of the faith, the history of the 'undivided' early church will be able to offer a firm basis for a common understanding of the Christian faith. In this way, one constructs, in fact, a more or less unspoiled constitutive phase in the history of the church which, for example, starting from a kind of principium quinque-saecularis, is restricted to the first five centuries (saecula) of the church or, at the most, extended to the first seven ecumenical councils[6].

This approach, however, also raises a great many questions, questions which are certainly familiar in Faith and Order circles. For example, in the report on "Patristic Studies from an Ecumenical Viewpoint" adopted at the Faith and Order Bristol meeting (1967), it is observed very soberly:

Hope: Commission on Faith and Order Accra 1974 (Faith and Order Paper No. 72), Geneva 1975, 25-80 and *Sharing in One Hope: Commission on Faith and Order Bangalore 1978* (Faith and Order Paper, No. 92), Geneva 1978, 1-11 en 51-202.

[5] Cf. Ch.S. Song (ed.), *Confessing our Faith around the World*, Vol.I (Faith and Order Paper No. 104), Geneva 1981 and H.G. Link (ed.), *Confessing our Faith around the World*, Vol.II (Faith and Order Paper No. 120), Geneva 1983; Vol.III: The Caribbean and Central America (Faith and Order Paper No. 123), Geneva 1984 and Vol.IV: South America (Faith and Order Paper No. 126) Geneva 1985.

[6] Cf. *Baptism, Eucharist & Ministry 1982-1990*, 133/134 with an explicit reference to the Russian Orthodox Church. In addition to the Councils of Nicea (325), Constantinople (381), Ephesus (431) and Chalcedon (451) the churches of East and West unanimously recognize three other councils as ecumenical: Constantinople II (553), Constantinople III (680-81) and Nicea II (787). In the Eastern church no council held after the separation of the West in 1054 received the title 'ecumenical'.

> *"The first centuries were certainly not a golden age, and the Early Church Fathers had no different task from what we have today, namely, the transmission of the apostolic message. Nevertheless they embody the 'primitive' tradition of the Church from which we all come"*[7].

As a continuation of this study, the Faith and Order Louvain meeting (1971) was presented with the report on "the Council of Chalcedon and its Significance for the Ecumenical Movement". This report, too, formulates a strikingly 'businesslike' approach to this council which was so important for the development of the christological dogma. The question of the range of influence of the Roman Emperor on the content of the decision of the council is unambiguously addressed:

> *"a) To what extent did this role influence the content of the decision of the Council? Was this role restricted to a simple direction of the agenda (e.g. pressure towards the production of a doctrinal definition) or did it reach the substance of the definition itself? To what extent was the concern for the unity of the Empire determinative for the Council? Was it important only for the formulation of certain canons or was it also a motivation in formulating the doctrine itself?*
> *b) What was the primary imperial concern (motive) in this Council? Was it only or mainly the concern for maintaining one faith in one Empire? Or should we see other political aims behind it?*
> *c) Was Chalcedon influenced by imperial intervention more than previous Councils?*
> *d) What was the importance of the fact that the faith of Chalcedon had, as in other cases, to be promulgated by special imperial decrees?*[8]

Apart from the political factors there is also a sensitivity in this report to the role played by the rivalry of the great ecclesiastical sees at the background of the council. What was the importance for Chalcedon of the particular interest of such sees as Rome,

---

[7] Cf for the text of this report, G. Gassmann (ed.), *Documentary History*, 218-225, esp. 219.
[8] Cf. for the text of the report, "The Council of Chalcedon and its Significance for the Ecumenical Movement", G. Gassmann (ed.), *Documentary History*, 226-235, esp. 227/228.

Constantinople, Alexandria, Antioch and the emerging Patriar-chate of Jerusalem? There is also the issue of the extent to which ethnic and cultural factors played a role in the history of Chal-cedon.

All these questions make it clear that, even with regard to the creeds of the ancient church, the question of the mediating role of the context cannot be shirked[9].

Bangalore 1978

When, at the Faith and Order Conference at Bangalore (1978), it was decided to strive for the formulation of a common under-standing of the apostolic faith by means of a separate study project, there was a deep awareness of the limited range of a doctrinal formulation of faith. This was perhaps inspired, at least in part, by the final results of the study project, "Giving Account of the Hope", presented at Bangalore. Hence, there was an explicit request for attention to be given to the distinction between faith as personal commitment and a doctrinal formula-tion:

> *"We are agreed that we must distinguish between faith as com-mitment and the doctrinal formulation of faith. Faith as the human response to the grace of God, as commitment with love and hope, is essential. The attempt to give it a doctrinal formulation is sec-ondary to it. Therefore, every statement of faith must be recog-nized as limited in scope, expression and relevance. It cannot itself become the object of our faith"* [10].

---

[9] See for this mediating context e.g. the contributions by A. Heron on "The Historically Conditioned Character of the Apostles' Creed" (20-26) and by C. Kannengiesser on "Nicaea 325 in the History of Christendom" (27-35) in the special issue of *Concilium* 118 (1978) on "An Ecumenical Confession of Faith?". See also the monumental work by A. Grillmeier, *Jesus Christus im Glauben der Kirche*, Vol. I: Von der apostolischen Zeit bis zum Konzil von Chalcedon (451), Freiburg 1990[3] and for a concise description of both the content and context of Nicea and Chalcedon, J.N.D. Kelly, *Early Christian Doctrines*, London 1980[5].

[10] G. Gassmann (ed.), *Documentary History*, 31.

The direction in which one was thinking at Bangalore also becomes clear in the doxology which was articulated there and then. Growing together in one faith, the divided Christian communities declared themselves to be already prepared to share a doxology taken from our common heritage, the Scriptures. They point especially to one passage which summarizes many aspects of our common confession, Ephesians 1: 3-15. Together with this doxology they state:

> *"We confess God's involvement in the history of humankind, revealed through Israel, fulfilled in Jesus Christ, communicated to us by the Holy Spirit, into which fulfilment all humanity is called; we confess the destiny and dignity of all **human beings**, rooted in God's initiative and design;*
> *we confess our dependence upon **God's redeeming and liberating grace**, because we are caught up in the ambiguities of our history and because we live in sin;*
> *we confess the reality of the **Event of Jesus Christ** – his life, his death, his resurrection – and the reality of our answer of faith, given to that Event, that brings us, through the Spirit, to the incorporation into Christ, which means our salvation;*
> *we confess the reality of **the Church**, being the Body of Christ, called to be the nucleus and servant of the unity of humankind and of the universe. We confess our responsibility as Christians to have the mind of Christ and to live and act accordingly in the community of humankind; faith without work is dead;*
> *we confess the presence and the working of the **Spirit**, the pledge and seal of the kingdom, into which we are confirmed"* [11].

When, however, the Faith and Order consultation at Odessa in 1981 opted for the explication of the creed of Nicea-Constantinople of 381 as the only creed shared by churches of the Eastern and Western traditions[12], at least two things became clear[13].

---

[11] See for the complete text of this "Common Statement of Our Faith", G. Gassmann (ed.), *Documentary History*, 169-170, esp. 170.

[12] A. Falconer refers to this meeting at Odessa as a consultation "which brought together an equal representation of Orthodox and non-Orthodox, but where the interests of Africa, Asia and Latin America were not well represented". See A. Falconer, "En Route to Santiago", 49.

[13] Cf. for the text of the Odessa report on "The Ecumenical Importance of the Nicene Creed", H.G. Link (ed.), *Apostolic Faith Today: A Handbook for Study* (Faith and Order Paper No. 124), Geneva 1985, 245-256.

In the first place there was no option for a more contemporary attempt at interpreting the apostolic faith, something which might yet have been considered as following naturally from the study project, "Giving Account of the Hope". There was an explicit choice for a distinctly historical approach. In this connection, in view of the surprisingly new contextual initiative of the 'Giving Account of the Hope' programme, Alan Falconer now speaks of a "missed opportunity" and concludes that the study project, "Giving Account of the Hope", has become a forgotten byway en route from Montreal[14].

And in the second place, a certain historical fixation seems, in this way, to serve indeed as a criterion of faith for subsequent generations, whereas the reference to the Montreal concept of tradition enables one to apply a far more dynamic concept of faith. The fact that, for many people, the Nicene-Constantinopolitan Creed is much more than "the theological and methodological tool" towards the explication of the apostolic faith certainly appears from the final sentence of that section in the "Introduction" to the final document, *Confessing the One Faith*, in which the choice of this confession is justified:

[14] A. Falconer, "En Route to Santiago", 49: "In its study project, 'Giving Account of the Hope that Is within Us', the Commission had gathered contemporary expressions of the Christian faith from a wide variety of cultures. Some of these confessions had been the officially approved statements of churches attempting to articulate the faith for their specific contemporary situation, for example, those of the Kimbanguist Church, the Presbyterian Church in Cuba, and the Presbyterian Church in Taiwan, while others had arisen from the reflection of individuals and groups. A rich tapestry was woven. The diversity of expressions of the faith, together with the intercontextual method adopted by the Commission, suggested that the question posed at Montreal by Ernst Käsemann concerning the diversity of the church might become a focus of enquiry in the search for the unity of the church. Käsemann had stressed the fact that, for the New Testament, the church perceived unity *through*, rather than *despite*, diverse structures, liturgies and expressions of faith. Thus the church could be perceived as a koinonia (community) of churches which manifest and articulate the gospel in their various cultural contexts. In the event, the opportunity was missed and the exercise of 'Giving Account of the Hope that Is within Us' has become a forgotten byway en route from Montreal". See for the text of Käsemann's conference address, E. Käsemann, "Unity and Diversity in New Testament Ecclesiology", *Novum Testamentum* 6 (1963) 290-297.

"The Nicene Creed thus serves to indicate whether the faith as set forth in modern situations is the same as the one the Church confessed through the centuries" [15].

Clearly, this creed has been introduced as a criterion for authentic apostolic faith. That does not, however, imply that, from now on, every tension between historical continuity and topical relevance will be avoided in this study project. It is explicitly acknowledged that the search for a common historical basis is only one single component of the common witness of the churches. There is also another component which consists in searching for a common answer to the challenges of our modern culture. That is indeed the reason why a dual task is formulated:

"In order to respond to their calling, churches which belong to different Christian traditions and live in diverse cultural, social, political and religious contexts, need to reappropriate their common basis in the apostolic faith so that they may confess their faith together".

However, apart from this, it is also accepted that:

"The apostolic faith must always be confessed anew and interpreted in the context of changing times and places" [16].

A natural consequence of this awareness of the need for actualization is the concern to indicate the relevance of the basic convictions of the Christian faith in the face of the particular *challenges* of our time and world. With a view to this end, the hope is that it might be possible to formulate *basic insights* which can be understood and accepted by Christians from different traditions.

Lima 1982

The report, "Towards the Common Expression of the Apostolic Faith Today", which was adopted by the Faith and Order meeting

---

[15] *Confessing the One Faith*, 4.

[16] See the "Introduction" in: *Confessing the One Faith: An Ecumenical Explication of the Apostolic Faith at it is Confessed in the Nicene-Constantinopolitan Creed (381)* (Faith and Order Paper No. 153), Geneva 1991, 1-9, esp. 2.

in Lima, makes it clear just how seriously the challenge to be made to the traditional creed were taken. For example, the following challenges are formulated there:

> "The Ecumenical Creed confesses the faith in one God. ... What does faith in one God mean for human community torn by poverty, militarism, racism?
>
> The Ecumenical Creed confesses faith in one Lord, Jesus Christ. How do we explicate that to contemporaries in a myriad of cultural and religious situations who, venerating Jesus, understand him to be a mere human being? Or who refuse to see his lordship in social, economic, political life?
>
> The Ecumenical Creed confesses that Jesus Christ was crucified for us under Pontius Pilate. How do we make clear to our contemporaries that salvation has a historical character, that it is no mere cosmological speculation, but a matter of divine election and mission to all humanity? How do we proclaim God's coming into human suffering in the cross, strengthening and empowering as well as consoling those who are oppressed by sin and evil?
>
> The Ecumenical Creed confesses the life of the age to come. How can we explain to twentieth century neighbours an understanding of life which transcends death, yet can be lived now? How can we explicate a Christian hope, rooted and grounded in eternal life with God, which addresses urgent human problems, which illumines human suffering and persecution, which clarifies and judges human utopias in the light of the coming kingdom?[17].

The question of whether the Nicene Creed can be considered 'sufficient' to express the Christian faith for contemporary Christians is explicitly raised several other times in this report. It is indeed pointed out that some biblical themes and concepts, indispensable for Christian life and thought, are not explicitly treated in the Creed, not to mention the meaning of Jesus' concrete words and actions, about which nothing is said by the old ecumenical symbols of faith. Moreover, it is also acknowledged that many Christians legitimately ask whether confessing the faith of the Creed of Nicea means being bound to ancient Greco-Roman forms of thought and speech.

---

[17] See for the text of this report, G. Gassmann (ed.), *Documentary History*, 191-200, esp. 196/197.

Must God remain Greek?

This question is ever more forcefully raised from Africa, and most clearly articulated by Robert Hood in his study *Must God remain Greek?*:

> *"Today it seems enormously important that Christianity be able to disentangle its religious selfunderstanding from its Greek patrimony. Despite its monumental contributions, the classical legacy now threatens the survival and integrity of Christian identity in this world of many and varied cultures, where even fellow Christians bear far different assumptions than their Euro-American counterparts about what is good, beautiful, and even real"* [18].

Hood relates his criticism of Greco-Roman dominance directly to the World Council study project, *Confessing the one Faith.* He is aware that the church revised tenets borrowed from Greek and Roman philosophical thought. Nonetheless, its doctrines continue to reflect ethnocentric philosophical ideas about the absolute, unchanging nature and transcendence of the divine, about how the divine can be related to flux and change in creation and humankind, and about the need to concoct a way of allying Greek thought with biblical thought about God and Jesus Christ. Such an alliance – so Hood argues – *ipso facto* today not only excludes the possible intellectual contribution and integrity of ancient African cultures south of the Sahara in conversations about Christ and the Spirit, but also establishes the agenda that determines how the worldview of these African cultures will be heard by the guardians of traditions. Hence – Hood asks – might it not be said that the political concept of 'neocolonialism' is also an appropriate charge to raise with regard to the Eurocentric guardianship and control of the Christian tradition? With respect to content, the Afro cultures would have to raise the following key questions:

[18] Cf. Robert E. Hood, *Must God remain Greek? Afro Cultures and God-Talk*, Minneapolis 1990, XI.

> *"First, what might doctrines about Christ and the Spirit look like*
> *if the concepts and intellectual frame of reference of Afro cultures*
> *– instead of Graeco-Roman thought – were used as vehicles for*
> *interpreting biblical narratives and views in the formation of*
> *Christian doctrine?*
> *Second, Christian doctrine about Christ has primarily focused on*
> *the issue of **cur deus homo?** – that is, on how Jesus Christ could*
> *be both human and God – and, once that puzzle is worked out, it*
> *has focused on the relationship of the God-man to our salvation*
> *and redemption as sinful humankind. God-talk in Afro cultures,*
> *however, asks: What is the significance of this redemption for cre-*
> *ation and nature, where good and evil powers, forces, and princi-*
> *palities reign and shape the human situation?*
> *Third, since the founding of the World Council of Churches in*
> *Amsterdam in 1948, Eurocentric and American churches have*
> *moved and controlled the modern ecumenical movement, declar-*
> *ing as a universal Christian goal the 'restoration of visible unity in*
> *one faith' among Christian churches. Yet God-talk in Afro cultures*
> *raises the serious question: What will be the nature of that unity,*
> *worthy as it might be in our fragmented ecclesiastical and politi-*
> *cal world?*[19]

In the theological review of the World Council of Churches, the American Eastern-Orthodox theologian Stanley Harakas gave a direct reaction to Hood's challenging book by answering the question "Must God remain Greek?" in a threefold manner, namely: "No! Yes! and Somehow!".

With regard to his "No!", Harakas acknowledges that no system of thought, no human categories, no cultural expressions, no human words, no art, no symbols, can fully capture the being of God for us. God is not Greek. Nor is God Korean, European, Australian, white, black or yellow, male or female. Everyone who reflects on God must stand in awe before God's total holy otherness. To call God "holy" precisely means that we acknowledge God's transcendence. The Scriptures themselves *use* Hebrew and

---

[19] R.E. Hood, *Must God remain Greek?*, 247/248. After the reading of the section on "The concept of koinonia" in chapter I, it will be obvious to the reader that Hood here slightly caricaturizes the ideal of unity within the World Council of Churches. Koinonia specifically presupposes diversity, as the discussion in chapter I indicated.

Greek. In themselves the Hebrew culture and the Greek culture are not sources of revelation, not redemptive, not adequate for the renewal of the cosmos, and so on.

With regard to his "Yes!", however, Harakas stresses that these particular cultures provided the outward form for the expression of God's revelation in Jesus Christ. There is this Hebrew/Greek particularity which cannot simply be replaced by any other. However, if 'God is Greek' in this sense, it is an external identification. After all, we are told that in Christ, "there is neither Jew, nor Greek" (Gal.3:28).

Hence, Harakas speaks of "Somehow!". If, for example the doctrine of the Trinity or of the two natures of Jesus Christ is Greek, it is a Greek which has been scooped out and packed full of a new meaning, a Christian meaning. The Christian message must be incarnated in the languages, cultures and mind-sets of all people, *using* every possible cultural expression to convey this saving message. But the struggle here is always how to acknowledge the integrity of the given character of the revelation while being able to incarnate it in every human condition. Seeking to incarnate the Gospel in culture may, in the end, result in the substitution of culture for the Gospel. Every tradition contains nation and culture elements which are opposed to the Gospel. There are beliefs and practices that are not compatible with the fundamental affirmations of the Christian faith.

Pointing to these three positions, "No!", "Yes!" and "Somehow!", Harakas's position can be summarized in these phrases: "There is a core of Christian truth that is to be found expressed in the shell of a culture. It is historically what it is. It is there, in the Greek scriptures and the early Christian tradition, that the tradition of revelation is to be found. There is no other. There is no substitute for it. But it is a message and 'way' that must itself be incarnated in every culture and nation and people (including that of modern-day Greeks) and for all persons in the lived reality of their concrete experience"[20].

---

[20] S.S. Harakas, "Must God remain Greek?", *The Ecumenical Review* 43 (1991) 194-199, esp. 199.

Apostolic faith

Within this study project, the possibility of surmounting the gap between past and present is given in in the highly dynamic interpretation of the term Tradition as formulated by Montreal and as applied in the Lima texts to the concept of apostolic faith. That interpretation of apostolic faith is also explicitly endorsed in the study project, *Confessing the One Faith:*

> *"Apostolic faith refers not to a single fixed formula, nor to a specific moment in Christian history. Rather, it points to the dynamic reality of the Christian faith. This faith is grounded in the prophetic witness of the people of the Old Testament, and in the normative testimony, reflected in the New Testament, of the apostles and those who proclaimed together with them the gospel in the early days (apostolic age) and in the testimony of their community. The apostolic faith is expressed in confession, in preaching, in worship and in the sacraments of the Church as well in the credal statements, decisions of councils and confessional texts and in the life of the church"* [21].

In the light of the above-mentioned view of apostolic faith, and the position assigned to the Nicene-Constantinopolitan Creed in the articulation of this faith, one might indicate the meaning of the term 'apostolic faith' in World Council of Churches' documents in the following six points:

1. The identity of the church depends on its continuity with the apostolic tradition.

2. Within the multifaceted apostolic tradition, the apostolic faith is foundational for the identity of the church.

3. Apostolicity is a dynamic reality, consisting in the presence of Christ as confessed by his followers.

4. Unity in the apostolic faith exists in the pluriformity of Christian traditions in a great diversity of contexts.

5. In the quest for the common expression of the apostolic faith, the churches are asked to recognize the Nicene-Constanti-

---

[21] *Confessing the One Faith*, 2/3. This text has been derived from a "preliminary working definition" articulated at a consultation in Rome in 1983 and quoted by H.G. Link (ed.), *Apostolic Faith Today*, 266.

nopolitan creed as the ecumenical symbol (i.e., confessional document) *par excellence*.

6. The fundamental criterion (*norma normans*) of apostolicity
lies in the consonance of our faith with the testimony of the apostles to God's revelation in Jesus Christ as recorded in the Scriptures[22].

One may wonder, however, whether this dynamization of the
concept of tradition is not again undone, when it is concluded that
the central affirmations of the apostolic faith were set out in a particular way in the credal statements of the early church, and, in
particular, in the Ecumenical Creed of Nicea and Constantinople
(381). As opposed to other creeds of regional authority three arguments are produced in favor of the Nicene-Canstantinopolitan
Creed:

– it has been more universally received than any other symbol
of the faith, as a normative expression of the essential content of
the apostolic faith;

– it is part of the historical heritage of contemporary Christianity;

– it has been in liturgical use through the centuries to express
the one faith of the Church[23].

Failed Challenges

One might wonder whether one specific confession is not, after
all, given too much weight here, and put in a position too close to the
gospel itself. This creed, too, has after all been articulated in the
midst of a rather great diversity and also, in a sense, implies a nar-
rowing down of the apostolic tradition. Should not, therefore, this
creed itself also be tested regularly against the question of whether it

---

[22] See for these six points, G. Vandervelde, "The Meaning of 'Apostolic Faith' in
World Council of Churches' Documents", 25.
[23] *Confessing the One Faith*, 4.

really leaves room for legitimate diversity within the apostolic tradition, instead of acting as a criterion itself?[24]

The fact that the creeds of the early church have a certain surplus value with respect to the later creeds may be defended on the basis of the argument that an initial period is always to a greater extent constitutive for a tradition – in the sense of: serving as a verifying point – than later periods that are further removed from that initial period. This does not, however, raise the initial period above the ambiguity accompanying all history. Historical-critical research, therefore, should also cover the history of the early church, and what is specific in these creeds can only be traced by studying them explicitly in the light of the historical, political and social context from which they originated. In this way, the permanent value of the witness of the faith articulated in the creeds of the early church is done more justice than in a seemingly unproblematic reception.

In view of the report on Chalcedon and the challenges which were most penetratingly formulated in Lima, however, one may also wonder whether there has not been a shift of accent within this study project through the years. Since the moment when a choice was made in favour of the Nicene Creed, those who raised the question of actualization most cogently, seem to have dissociated themselves somewhat disappointedly from the project. At the same time, those who remained involved in the project (Tillard, Pannenberg, Tanner, Deschner, Kühn, Wainwright et al.), particularly in reaction to African criticism of the 'Greek' conceptuality

---

[24] The extent to which Faith and Order, during the study project, *Confessing the One Faith,* has come to put this creed ever more explicitly alongside Scripture and Tradition (with a capital T) appears, for example, from the following phrase in *Confessing the One Faith,* 5: "Accordingly, the explication will seek to respond to the question as to what degree and in which form the fundamentals of the apostolic faith as witnessed by the Holy Scriptures, proclaimed in the Tradition of the Church, and expressed in the Creed, can be commonly understood and expressed by churches of different, confessional traditions, living in different cultural, social, economical, political and religious contexts". For the debate regarding, among other things, this state of affairs, see especially the bibliography in *Confessing the One Faith,* 121-124.

of the creed and the problems of many Western theologians with
the substance of the creed, have become more and more sensitive
to the historicizing approach of Eastern Orthodoxy[25].

One may even wonder whether the study project, *Confessing
the One Faith,* in the form in which it has now been concluded, is
not a step backward behind the hermeneutic viewpoints which
have been articulated within Faith and Order with respect to the
relation Scripture-Tradition. With regard to the question of a
hermeneutics of the apostolic tradition within Faith and Order, it
was explicitly declared that the ecumenical dialogue itself can be
seen as a unique opportunity for the hermeneutic process to take

---

[25] Geoffrey Wainwright, for example, observes the following about Wolfhart Pannenberg, one of his fellow participants in the steering group of this study project:
"Later in that year in Bangalore, and then again in 1982 in Lima, he was among
those who fought hardest in the plenary commission meetings of Faith and Order
for making the Nicene-Constantinopolitan Creed the 'basis and instrument' of the
resultant Faith and Order study 'Towards the Common Expression of the Apostolic Faith Today'. This procedure imposed itself over the problems Western lib-
erals have with the substance of the creed, and over the difficulties many Africans
in particular have with its 'Greek' conceptuality. ... There may have taken place a
slight shift of emphasis on Pannenberg's part as the true colors of liberalism
became more evident to him. He has always maintained that 'personal confession
of Jesus' (*Bekenntnis zu Jesus*) suffices for access to the Church and its sacraments. Already in a paper of 1973 on 'Confessions and the Unity of Christians',
however, he recognized that, as early as the New Testament period itself, willing-
ness to use the language of the Church *of the time* was a necessary test in order to
ensure that the would-be believer intended the object of the Church's proclamation (e.g., Mark 8,29; Rom.10,9; I Cor.12,3 and I John 4,15). Pannenberg's enthusiasm for the Nicene-Constantinopolitan Creed may betoken a deeper appreciation
for the *diachronic continuity* needed at the linguistic level – somewhat along the
lines of the Church as a cultural-linguistic tradition ... – in order to maintain the
identity of the Church's message and faith. It may also show a greater sensitivity
to the need to make explicit the trinitarian dimensions of 'confession of Jesus'".
Cf. G. Wainwright, "Pannenberg's Ecumenism" in: C.E. Braaten/Ph. Clayton
(eds.), *The Theology of Wolfhart Pannenberg: Twelve American Critiques, with
an Autobiographical Essay and Response*, Minneapolis 1988, 207-223, esp. 211.
Cf. for an analysis of Pannenberg's more pluralistic 'early' ecclesiology, M.E.
Brinkman, "De plaats van de kerk in W. Pannenbergs theologie. Een beknopte
verkenning in zijn ecclesiologie", *Nederlands Theologisch Tijdschrift* 32 (1978)
31-41 and in a more extensive version under the title, "De kerk en het vraagstuk
der pluriformiteit in de theologie van Wolfhart Pannenberg" in: T. Baarda e.a.
(red.), *Segmenten. Studies op het gebied van de theologie*, Amsterdam 1978, 1-27.

place under the commonly acknowledged authority of God's word. The paradosis of the gospel is received within a continuous rereading, reception and reappropriation of the narrative of God's salvation (see the end of chapter I).

The ecumenical movement itself may therefore be regarded as one large, open and dynamic depositum fidei. The confessions of the church of the centuries are here, as it were, deposited, preserved and studied and here new confessions of faith are continually gathered from all the continents and analyzed. Such a depositum fidei, as a never to be closed depot of faith, would, in a way, resemble what, in the history of European Lutheranism and Calvinism, was called a *harmonia confessionum*. In this, the confessions of faith of the church of all centuries and places might be put alongside each other. It would be the task of Faith and Order to analyze all those texts as to their consensus catholicus. Only in such a dynamic process of transmission will the true consensus catholicus become manifest in the creeds, the liturgy and the concrete social concerns of contemporary Christianity.

In my view, the present conclusion of the study project, *Confessing the One Faith*, namely, an interpretation of the Nicenum which, to some extent, is brought up to date, represents only the beginning. Too little justice has been done, as yet, to the challenge of the far-reaching inculturation of the Christian faith in Africa, Asia and Latin America.

There is every indication, however, of the fact that the contextualization of the articulation of faith, manifesting itself in these continents, will continue even more strongly during the next decades. After several decades of political struggle against Western domination in many different forms of liberation theology, the time now seems to have come for many Christians in Africa, Asia and Latin America to themselves formulate the deepest motives of their own faith in images derived from their own culture. That tendency, at least, was clearly visible at the Seventh World Assembly of the World Council of Churches at Canberra in 1991 and recently in 1993 during the Fifth World Conference of Faith and Order at Santiago de Compostela. This development will have far-reaching consequences for the worldwide ecumenical discussion. The centuries-old Western regionalization of the discussion of faith, which we from the West liked to pass off as the universal discussion of faith, will now at least be matched by all kinds of *other* regionalizations from Asia, Africa and Latin America[26].

Such a regionalization does not necessarily imply a threat to the unity of world Christianity. In the first place, that unity is presently not as intense as is sometimes suggested and, in the second place, the possibility does not have to be ruled out in advance that a problem which seemed to be typical of one continent will, after all, mutatis mutandis, emerge as an urgent problem in another. For example, for decades, we, as Europeans, have considered tribalism a typically African problem. Now, as African theologians are quick to point out, Europe, too, is witnessing one tribal war after another, some of which are religiously motivated.

Contextualization and Inculturalization

The new challenge of this aspect of the ecumenical movement lies mainly in taking the consequences of this contextuality seriously. The concept of contextuality serves to refer to the complicated process in which culture, religion, tradition and community

---

[26] Cf. A. Houtepen, "Discussie en reflectie over 'Geloof en kerkorde: De vijfde wereldconferentie te Santiago de Compostela in 1993", *Tijdschrift voor Theologie* 33 (1993) 390-403, esp. 401 where, as one of the new perspectives of this World Conference, he points to the attention for 'ecumenism per region' and the question arising from it of 'a more differentiated dialogue'. In this connection he also points to the great attention of the Pontifical Council for Promoting Christian Unity for the "Complexity and Diversity of the Ecumenical Situation" in the new *Directory for the Application of Principles and Norms of Ecumenism*, Vatican City 1993, 23/24 (Chapter I, No. 30-34). See for the relation gospel-culture at Canberra especially the address of the Korean feminist theologian, Chung Hyun Kyung on the theme of the assembly "Come, Holy Spirit – Renew the Whole Creation" in: M. Kinnamon (ed.), *Signs of the Spirit: Official Report Seventh Assembly*, Geneva 1991, 37-47 and 92/93, 98 and 102 (remarks in the Section Reports) and also the reactions from the side of the Eastern-Orthodox and the Evangelicals, 279-282 and 282-285 respectively. Cf. further the evaluating issue of *The Ecumenical Review* 43 (1991) No. 2.

are interrelated. The concept came to be used from the early seventies onwards as a contrastive concept over against indigenization. In the latter term many theologians from Africa, Asia and Latin America appeared to detect paternalism and the stigmatization of non-Western cultures on the basis of Western generalizations. It is true that the term indigenization, in the history of the missionary movement, implied new and serious attention to the plurality of cultures. However, this attention was still too much dominated by the project of the one, coherent world Christianity expanding from the West.

As opposed to this, the concept of contextualization emphasizes exclusively the unique function of non-Western expressions of faith and theology within the one history of God in relation to humanity. In this way, the universal validity of Western paradigms is fundamentally contested. Hence, the concept acquires a polemic accentuation. In ecumenical debates on 'mission' and particularly also in the various forms of liberation theology, this concept now represents an approach in which communication on the subject of faith and theology is necessarily connected with the tension between particular (local) experience and universal (world-wide) pretension.

It will be evident that the concept of contextuality also easily fits into social, economic and political relations. Fundamentally, the concept also points to the interrelatedness of all these factors. There is no theological speech that can escape this interrelatedness. One always finds oneself in a network of thought, speech and action where the exercise of power is a reality. It is precisely this which demands conscious reflection. Hence, Western theology should always be called to take its own contextuality seriously.

Of late the concept of contextuality seems to have been increasingly replaced by the concept of inculturation. Thereby, at first sight, a less militant concept seems to have been introduced, since the concept of contextuality – as has just been argued – always contains something of emancipation and liberation, of acknowledgment of the legitimate place of one's own context, whereas inculturation evokes far more harmonious associations. That is also the reason why these two words sometimes find themselves confronting each other in the debates as shibboleths in the struggle between cultural and political (liberation) theology. However, such a fixation does not necessarily have to accompany the concepts themselves.

In the concept of inculturation it is always a matter of two aspects: faith, or the Gospel, is integrated with a culture on a fundamental level, while also having a critical transforming effect in it. Thus, in an ongoing process of inculturation, faith also finds new forms of expression which, in their turn, may also create unity. Therefore, the plurality of the Christian faith, claimed in the concepts of contextuality and inculturation, does not by definition have to stand in the way of the (renewed) unity in faith.

In order to prevent the struggle (for power) which is so inextricably bound up with the concept of contextuality from being pushed completely into the background, it is probably advisable to continue to distinguish more interests within the concept of inculturation, namely a translation interest, an adaptation interest and a liberation interest:

What is at stake in a translation interest is the concern for the integrity of a message which has to be transferred to different cultural situations and has, therefore, to be translated. Here, attention to culture and socio-political problems is easily instrumentalized for the sake of proclamation.

What is at stake in an adaptation interest is the harmonious development of the one constant tradition in the various cultures.

A liberation interest concerns the quest for authentic expression of faith and is dominated by directly experienced problems of alienation and oppression.

It will be evident that the exciting discussions within the World Council of Churches and within the Roman Catholic Church on the relationship between Gospel and culture concern, above all, the third interest. The sometimes clearly noticeable fear of this form of inculturation frequently seems to disregard God's promise to the church of all times and places, that He and his Spirit will never forsake the church. Greater confidence in this promise of God might create a far less prejudiced basis for the discussion of faith between North and South and East and West than some people, whose faith is perhaps described in Matt.17:20, now believe to be possible[27].

The realization is slowly but surely gaining ground that, in overcoming divisions within the Church in many parts of the world, common confession of faith would involve much more than agreement on creeds and church orders. It would involve dealing with divisions arising out of non-theological factors, such as cultural and socio-political circumstances. Therefore, it would mean an understanding of the relationship between Gospel and culture as well as between Gospel and power structures. Since, in many of the third world countries the Church constitutes a minority, this search has to be undertaken along with people of other faiths and non-believers.

The fundamental and novel character of the questions that are to be raised here is evident in one of the section reports of the Fifth World Conference on Faith and Order in Santiago de Compostela (1993). The influence of those themes which recur in the dialogue with the other world religions is reflected in questions such as the following:

> *"Can cultures themselves, as part of God's good creation, be bearers and revealers of God's truth **in their very particularity**? To what extent is the Word, the one who 'was in the beginning', actively present among those who have not yet heard the Gospel proclaimed?"*

With reference to these questions it is observed that:

> *"Increasingly, some argue that God has indeed been present in their cultures, divine gifts offered and divine goodness revealed, even before missionaries arrived with formal teaching and preaching. To take this claim seriously is not only potentially to rethink our theological methodology, but also to rethink the meaning and nature of the tasks of mission and evangelism"* [28].

---

[27] See for the illuminating distinction between indigenization, contextualization and inculturation esp. B. Hoedemaker/A. Houtepen/Th. Witvliet, *Oecumene als leerproces. Inleiding in de Oecumenica*, Utrecht-Leiden 1993, 268-270.

[28] *Fifth World Conference on Faith and Order: Santiago de Compostela 1993: Message-Sections-Reports Discussion Paper*, 35 and Th.F. Best/G. Gassmann (eds.), *On the way to Fuller Koinonia*, 258.

Inextricably bound up with the further reflection on the cultural diversity of the Christian faith is also the question of the limits of this diversity. In the Canberra Statement on the Unity of the Church ("The Unity of the Church as Koinonia: Gift and Calling") diversity is said to be illegitimate when

> "it makes impossible the common confession of Jesus Christ as God and Saviour the same yesterday, today and forever (Heb.13:8); and salvation and the final destiny of humanity as proclaimed in holy scripture and preached by the apostolic community" [29].

During the Fifth World Conference on Faith and Order at Santiago four other criteria were added to this main criterion. These may be interpreted as implications of what has been stated above. Diversity can never be a reason for:

" – justifying discrimination on the basis of race or gender:
– preventing appropriate acts of reconciliation;
– hindering the common mission of the Church;
– endangering the life in koinonia" [30].

It will be clear, however, that the concrete application of these criteria will always depend on the degree to which one is prepared to engage mutual, continuous and compelling – in the sense of correcting – dialogue. Where that preparedness is lost, the basic Christian attitude towards koinonia is lost[31]. That is the reason why, in the document *Costly Unity*, drawn up for the Fifth World Conference on Faith and Order, Lukas Vischer rightly observes that, in the pathos with which one argues in favour of diversity, an unholy fire may also burn if unity is not simultaneously sought: "Why emphasize the need for diverse expressions of the faith without at the same time stressing the need for reconciliation and communication? We are living in a period of fragmentation and excessive pluralism. Communication is breaking down. Why not

---

[29] G. Gassmann (ed.), *Documentary History of Faith and Order*, 3-5, esp.4.
[30] *Fifth World Conference on Faith and Order*, 26 (text of the dicussion paper "Towards Koinonia in Faith, Life and Witness", nr. 57). See also Th.F. Best/G. Gassmann (eds.), *On the way to Fuller Koinonia*, 280.
[31] Cf. M. Kinnamon, *Truth and Community: Diversity and its Limits in the Ecumenical Movement*, Grand Rapids/Geneva 1988.

concentrate all energies on the task of showing new ways of establishing bridges of encounter and solidarity? How can God's covenant become manifest through the koinonia of the churches? Facing the disintegration of human society, the Faith and Order Commission will have to fulfil its constitutional task of keeping prominently before the churches God's call to unity"[32].

However, – as Douglas Hall inquired after the World Convocation on Justice, Peace and Integrity of Creation at Seoul (Korea) in 1990 – is it possible for churches which have (rightly!) begun to engage in theologies that are consciously contextual to work simultaneously towards a pertinent global confession of Christian faith today? The greatest frustration at Seoul was the failure to combine the quest for a globally appropriate profession of faith with commitments to theological and ethical positions that had been hammered out on the anvils of specific socio-historical contexts.

The challenge that Seoul presents to the churches is to manifest a form of *ecumenism* that is not just a stained-glass version of the *cosmopolitanism* of the universal homogeneous state. Therefore, we are looking for an ecumenism that treasures the variety of gifts that are brought, not only by individuals, but also by nations and peoples for the enrichment of the reign of God[33].

Confessing the One Faith

The above-mentioned critical comments on the study project, *Confessing the One Faith,* arise from the notion that any articulation of the Christian faith that claims to set universal criteria,

[32] L. Vischer, "Koinonia in a Time of Threats to Life" in: Th.F. Best/W. Granberg-Michaelson (eds.), *Costly Unity: Koinonia and Justice, Peace and Creation*, Geneva 1993, 70-82, esp. 79.
[33] Cf. D.J. Hall, "The State of the Ark: Lessons from Seoul" in: D.P. Niles (ed.), *Between the Flood and the Rainbow: Interpreting the Conciliar Process of Mutual Commitment (Covenant) to Justice, Peace and the Integrity of Creation*, Geneva 1992, 34-48, esp. 35 and 44.

should also effectively express the faith of world Christianity. Our main criticism is that, in the study project *Confessing the one Faith,* that is still insufficiently the case. This is, however, far from saying that this project would not in any sense be a step forward in the mutual recognition and acknowledgment of faith between the churches. On the contrary. The present final document presents an excellent illustration of present-day ecumenical Western theology. It offers nothing more, it is true, but certainly nothing less either.

This modern ecumenical theology is defined by a great number of valuable characteristics:

a) In this theology, one does not avoid the questioning of God raised by atheism and secularism, and one is not afraid of the discussion with the other religions.

b) In the doctrine of God, one is aware of the questioning of the concepts of father and omnipotence and one does not shun the question of theodicy.

c) In christology, one clearly senses the influence of historical-critical methods in New Testament exegesis and the processing of the results of modern dogma-historical research.

d) It is especially apparent in the description of the meaning of Jesus' death and resurrection and his proclamation of the kingdom of God that the liberation theologies of Asia, Africa and Latin America have left their mark.

e) As regards pneumatology, the ecumenical consensus which has grown in the discussion of faith with Eastern Orthodoxy has been incorporated. This discussion concerned the so-called 'filioque', the Spirit who, in the judgement of the Western Church, proceeds equally from the Father and from the Son (filioque), but who, in the judgement of the Eastern Church, has the Father alone as his real source. Moreover, the Spirit of God has also quite specifically been related to creation. This latter shift is now common to many theologies of creation[34].

---

[34] The link between creation and Spirit was especially evident in the material developed in preparation for the seventh World Assembly of the World Council of Churches at Canberra. Cf. *Come, Holy Spirit – Renew the Whole Creation: Giver of Life – Sustain your Creation!*, special issue of *The Ecumenical Review* 42

f) In ecclesiology, rightly treated under the heading of pneumatology, a great many of the conceptions crystallized within Faith and Order about catholicity, apostolicity and baptism (Lima text) have been integrated.

g) At the end of the document, *Confessing the One Faith*, it is quite apparent that there is a concern to maintain the relation between this study project and the preceding study project, *Giving Account of the Hope within us*. Here, the study at once acquires a far more direct tone and the great problems of the world seem to have been articulated far more penetratingly than in the preceding text. Dealing with the eschatological expectation of the resurrection of the dead and of "the life of the (world) age to come", there is the emphatic declaration that since we, as Christians, affirm our hope for this world, a hope which is grounded in belief in the Triune God, we reject any escape from this world and its problems. This is followed by examples of concrete rejections of such escapes:

> *"Affirming our trust in the future God has prepared for us, we reject any attempt to secure our future at the expense of the world, especially through the threat of either nuclear or ecological destruction.*
>
> *Affirming the presence of the yet future kingdom, we reject any understanding of God's coming kingdom which either separates the kingdom of the world and its life, or identifies the kingdom with any historical reality.*
>
> *Affirming God's faithfulness to his entire creation, we reject any impoverishment of our hope which blinds us to the wholeness of God's redemption of individuals, of human community, or of all creation.*
>
> *Affirming that Jesus Christ with his Spirit is God's Word by which all is judged and its ultimate meaning is disclosed, we reject that the powers that seem to rule history will finally determine its meaning and destiny"*.

(1990) No. 2 with contributions by G. Lemopoulos; J. Moltmann; A. Bittlinger; J. Breck; Ignatios IV; G.M. Jantzen; L. Vischer; M.E. Brinkman; R.E. Lechte and J. McDaniel. See further E. Castro (ed.), *To the Wind of God's Spirit: Reflections on the Canberra Theme*, Geneva 1990.

In opposition to these rejections a number of very concrete examples of Christian expectation of the future are formulated:

> " In the face of despair over the world, our hope refuses to acquiesce in things as they are.
> In the face of growing hopelessness, our hope will declare no situation or person beyond hope.
> In the face of oppression, our hope affirms that oppression will not remain forever.
> In the face of religious perspectives misused to justify political programmes, our hope affirms that the advent of the kingdom of God is not within our power but remains in the power of God's surprising initiative.
> In the face of unbearable pain, incurable disease, and irreversible handicap, our hope affirms the loving presence of Christ who can make possible what is impossible to human powers" [35].

Here we see the relevance of the pithy formula contained in the "Common Account of Hope" developed in Bangalore:

> "The Christian Hope is a resistance movement against fatalism" [36].

It is precisely these inspiring phrases, however, that illustrate how wrong it was to momentarily separate the more detailed explication of the creed from the concrete breeding-ground of hope in real life situations everywhere in the world.

.

---

[35] *Confessing the One Faith*, 103.
[36] See for the whole text, G. Gassmann (ed.), *Documentary History*, 161-168, esp. 166.

CHAPTER IV

BAPTISM

Bond of Unity

In Christian baptism what essentially matters is what makes a Christian a Christian. It is, therefore, clearly more than a celebration of birth or an initiation rite for the sake of marking formal membership of a church. There is nothing wrong with delight in the birth of a human child playing a part in a baptismal liturgy, and in the formal sense of the word, baptism is also a rite of initiation. However, this is still far from capturing the essence of baptism. Baptism is, above all, an invitation to share in the gift of grace of Christ's life, death and resurrection. At the same time, it is a promise on the part of the person to be baptized, or the latter's parents and the faithful community, to also enter effectively into the imitation of Christ. Hence, the Lima text also underlines that, in baptism, God's gift and the person's answer go together:

> "Baptism is both God's gift and our human response to that gift" [1].

In spite of the great differences which there are, for example, between the advocates of infant baptism or adult baptism and the widely divergent views of the relation baptism-confirmation and baptism-eucharist, baptism is still one of the most evident examples of ecumenical consensus. In baptism it is apparently most easy for believers to recognize one another as fellow Christians.

---

[1] *Baptism, Eucharist and Ministry*, 3 (B.8). Cf. also *Confessing the One Faith*, 94: "The gift of God granted in baptism requires in every instance the human *response of faith* if it is to impart reconciliation effectively. This is true in every case also for those who are not yet able to answer for themselves".

Hence, this consensus also resulted in one of the most concrete ecumenical achievements, namely, mutual acknowledgments of baptism and also, in fact, in acknowledgments of churches. Therefore, every attempt to arrive at a common ecumenical ecclesiology is also based on a 'baptismal ecclesiology'. That is the reason why, at the Fifth World Conference on Faith and Order in Santiago de Compostela, it was observed:

> *"Insofar as they recognize each other's baptisms, the churches may be at the start of developing a baptismal ecclesiology in which to locate other elements of shared belief and life"* [2].

Apart from this, the ecumenical agreement in the field of baptism is also one of the best examples of a really successful ecumenical discussion. Here, the arguments of a minority – the advocates of adult baptism – have been taken completely seriously and have also, to a great degree, determined the theology of baptism of the so-called 'mainstream' churches to such an extent that, for the content of the theology of baptism in the Lima text, it is, in the end, not so much infant baptism, as adult baptism which serves as a model. It was especially the Decree on Ecumenism (No. 22) of Vatican II which set the tone for the ecumenical discussion on baptism:

> *"By the sacrament of Baptism, whenever it is properly conferred in the way the Lord determined and received with the proper dispositions of soul, man becomes truly incorporated into the crucified and glorified Christ and is reborn to a sharing of the divine life, as the Apostle says: 'For you were buried together with him in baptism, and in him also rose again through faith in the working of God who raised him from the dead" (Col.2:12). Baptism, therefore, constitutes the sacramental bond of unity existing among all who through it are reborn"*.

With this declaration, Vatican II again resumes the old position which Augustine had adopted in the case against the Donatists, who rejected the 'baptism of heretics': it is only the character of baptism as a gift that makes baptism what it is, not the sanctity of

---

[2] *Fifth World Conference on Faith and Order*, 24. Cf. also Th.F. Best/G. Gassmann (eds.), *On the way to Fuller Koinonia*, 247.

the one who administers baptism or of the person to be baptized. The same train of thought even brought both the Reformers and the Roman Catholic Counter-Reformation to an identical line of conduct during the height of the Reformation. There was an acknowledgement of each other's baptism, even though in the judgement of many people at the time, it concerned the baptism of 'heretics'[3].

Baptism as an invitation and gift of God transcends human ecclesiological antitheses and is therefore in itself constitutiv of church. Where baptism is administered, the universal Church 'happens'. Hence, in the light of this acknowledgment of the unity in baptism it is also possible for Vatican II to speak of separated *"churches"* and *"ecclesial"* communities (*Decree on Ecumenism*, Nos. 19-22).

Meaning of Baptism

The mutual acknowledgement of the liturgical rite of baptism and the words pronounced there has been supplemented by a remarkably broad agreement regarding the theology of baptism. The study, *One Lord, One Baptism*, published in 1960, already manifests the line which was followed in the final Lima text on baptism[4]. In the Lima text the central meaning of baptism is formulated as follows:

> *"Baptism is the sign of new life through Jesus Christ. It unites the one baptized with Christ and with his people.*

These words, which are directly derived from the New Testament witness, are then elaborated more thematically in the concept of participation (1); conversion, pardoning and cleansing (2); gift of the spirit (3); incorporation into the Body of Christ (4) and sign of the Kingdom (5)[5]:

[3] Cf. A. Vanneste, "La sainteté et la foi du ministère et du sujet des Sacrements", *Ephemerides Theologicae Lovanienses* 39 (1963) 5-29.

[4] *One Lord, One Baptism* (Studies in Ministry and Worship), London 1960.

[5] See for the main aspects of an ecumenical theology of baptism M. Thurian's "Introduction" in: M. Thurian/G. Wainwright (eds.), *Baptism and Eucharist: Ecumenical Convergence in Celebration* (Faith and Order Paper No. 117), Geneva

1. "Baptism means participating in the life, death and resurrection of Jesus Christ. Jesus went down into the river Jordan and was baptized in solidarity with sinners in order to fulfil all righteousness (Matt.3:15). This baptism led Jesus along the way of the Suffering Servant, made manifest in his sufferings, death and resurrection (Mark 10:38-40 and 45). By baptism, Christians are immersed in the liberating death of Christ where their sins are buried, where the 'old Adam' is crucified with Christ, and where the power of sin is broken".

2. "The baptism which makes Christians partakers of the mystery of Christ's death and resurrection implies confession of sin and conversion of heart .... The New Testament underlines the ethical implications of baptism by representing it as an ablution which washes the body with pure water, a cleansing of the heart of all sin, and an act of justification (Heb.10:22; I Peter 3:21; Acts 22:16 and I Cor.6:11). Thus those baptized are pardoned, cleansed and sanctified by Christ, and are given as part of their baptismal experience a new ethical orientation under the guidance of the Holy Spirit".

3. "The Holy Spirit is at work in the lives of people before, in and after their baptism. It is the same Spirit who revealed Jesus as the Son (Mark 1:10-11) and who empowered and united the disciples at Pentecost (Acts 2). God bestows upon all baptized persons the anointing and the promise of the Holy Spirit, marks them with a seal and implants in their hearts the first instalment of their inheritance as sons and daughters of God".

4. "Administered in obedience to our Lord, baptism is a sign and seal of our common discipleship. Through baptism, Christians are brought into union with Christ, with each other and with the Church of every time and place. Our common baptism, which unites us to Christ in faith, is thus a basic bond of unity .... Therefore, our one baptism into Christ constitutes a call to the churches to overcome their divisions and visibly manifest their fellowship".

1983, 3-4. See further for the genesis of the Lima text on baptism, G. Wagner, "Baptism from Accra to Lima" and L.S. Mudge, "Convergence on Baptism" in: M. Thurian (ed.), *Ecumenical Perspectives on Baptism, Eucharist and Ministry* (Faith and Order Paper No. 116), Geneva 1983, 12-32, 33-45 and also 209-214 ("First Draft of an Ecumenical Agreement on Baptism"(1970)).

5. *"Baptism initiates the reality of the new life given in the midst of the present world .... It is a sign of the Kingdom of God and of the life of the world to come"* [6].

The Practice of Baptism

The main ideas of the theology of baptism formulated in the Lima text were, in fact, already formulated in the report "Baptism, Confirmation and Eucharist", presented in Louvain in 1971[7]. This report not only unfolds a theology of baptism, but also goes in search of a comprehensive approach with respect to the theology of baptism, in the midst of the great divergence of baptismal practices among the churches. The fact is that, despite the fundamental agreement with regard to the meaning of baptism, there are a great many differences in the baptismal practices of the churches.

In the Eastern tradition baptism and confirmation (chrismation) are administered in immediate succession, even when the recipient is an infant[8]. The initiation is then complete. The person baptized is at once admitted to the eucharist, without further ceremony. Here the question must be asked whether children are given sufficient opportunity of making for themselves the confession of faith made on their behalf at baptism.

In the Western tradition, baptism and the laying on of hands (confirmation) were separated at quite an early date. Whereas baptism could be performed by the priest, the laying on of hands was reserved to the bishop. This meant that some time usually between baptism and confirmation. Where the person baptized was an infant, the interval might cover several years. Confirmation thus gradually became independent of baptism, although the close connection

[6] *Baptism, Eucharist and Ministry*, 2/3 (B.2-7). See for a more explicitly biblical elaboration of this ecumenical theology of baptism, *Confessing the One Faith*, 91/92.
[7] Cf. G. Gassmann (ed.), *Documentary History*, 104-115. After the publication of the Lima text the main ideas have again been summarized in *Confessing the One Faith*, 90-96.

between the two was never completely forgotten. Confirmation came to mean strengthening by the gift of the Holy Spirit. Admission to eucharistic fellowship could take place either before or after confirmation. All Western churches face the problem of refusing to admit children to the eucharist even though they have been baptized.

Western practice leads to the question of whether the division of initiation into two related yet distinct sacramental acts does not prejudice the unique once-for-all character of baptism. The churches of the Reformation sought to reassert the sufficiency of baptism. Since they found no basis in Scripture for confirmation as a sacramental act, it was abandoned. Other reasons, however, led the churches of the Reformation to adopt an act similar to the sacramental act of confirmation[9]. Baptized children are not admitted to the eucharist until they are able to make for themselves the profession of faith made at baptism. Confirmation furnishes the occasion for this act: a service of worship is held in which baptism is recalled and the persons previously baptized make a public profession of faith and are consecrated for their service. From then on they are admitted to the eucharist. Nevertheless, the practice of this kind of confirmation presents a special problem. Confirmation normally takes place when children reach a given age. However, a great many young members are no longer motivated to make this act of profession, either because of their critical attitude towards the church as institution – often confirmation is considered only as an act of loyalty to the institute – or because of a less clearly developed awareness of necessity, since many churches have dropped their insistence on confirmation as an essential condition for admission to the eucharist. They accept indiscriminately all their baptized children to the eucharist[10].

[8] Cf. for the Orthodox interpretation of the chrismation rite C. Argenti, "Chrismation" in: M. Thurian (ed.), *Ecumenical Perspectives*, 46-67.

[9] See for the differences and current convergences between Protestants and Catholics with regard to the confirmation, K. Lehmann/W. Pannenberg (eds.), *The Condemnations of the Reformation Era: Do they still Divide?*, Minneapolis 1989, 117-123.

[10] See on these questions, D.R. Holeton, "Confirmation in the 1980s" in: M. Thurian (ed.), *Ecumenical Perspectives*, 68-89.

In Anglicanism the practice of episcopal confirmation was retained. It has always involved both the personal ratification by the candidate of the promises made on his behalf at baptism, and the laying on of hands with prayer for his strengthening by the gift of the Holy Spirit. It is regarded as the way of entrance into communicant status.

The churches of the Baptist tradition administer baptism only to those who make a profession of faith. They have no rite of chrismation or confirmation, but in some churches there is a laying on of hands upon those who have been baptized. In all cases those who have been baptized are admitted at once to the eucharist. Often the children of baptized parents are dedicated during a special service of worship.

In the midst of all these differences the multi-coloredness of the biblical witness regarding baptism, and the many variations in the baptismal practice of the early church are additional complicating factors.

Clearly the New Testament assumes the practice of baptism, though it does not speak of it systematically, nor provide us with incontestable historical evidence as to its origin and practice. What is said about baptism occurs in many different contexts and, therefore, only throws light on certain aspects of baptism in widely varied first century settings. Many questions we should like to have answered today receive no direct answers from the witness of the New Testament. No Church can therefore base its practice on New Testament evidence alone; tradition and history play a significant role in shaping the churches' practice and provide the way in which the New Testament is interpreted and understood. It is important to acknowledge this fact. Churches must exercise caution in their judgements of each other's practice and expose their own practice to the critical questions of others.

The variety of practice in the Ancient church is also evident. Clearly the evidence of the New Testament and of the early centuries does not require a uniform baptismal practice throughout the whole church. One and the same baptism may be administered in different ways within certain limits in one and the same church. This point is important not only for the ecumenical movement but also for new expressions appropriate to baptism in churches living in other cultural settings (e.g. Africa).

Results of the Ecumenical Dialogue

In the midst of all the variations, however, some lines may be indicated, on the basis of bible and tradition, on which there is profound agreement in the ecumenical discussion and which may be directive for ecumenical acknowledgments of baptism:

1. Baptism should be a congregational act, included in worship, in which God's invitation and gift in Christ are proclaimed and accepted. Since baptism is intimately connected with the corporate life and worship of the Church, it should normally be administered during public worship, so that the members of the congregation may be reminded of their own baptism and may welcome into their fellowship those who are baptized and whom they are committed to nurture in the Christian faith.

2. Adult baptism has to be regarded as the primary form of baptism. While the possibility that infant baptism was also practised in the apostolic age cannot be excluded, baptism upon personal profession of faith is the most clearly attested pattern in the New Testament. The liturgy for infant baptism has therefore been an adaptation of that primary form. The two liturgies should not differ fundamentally. Otherwise the impression can be created that adult and infant baptism are two different baptisms.

3. The liturgy of baptism should provide for the following elements:

a. Acknowledgement of God's initiative in salvation, of His continuing faithfulness, and of our total dependence upon His grace.

b. Explanation of the meaning of baptism as it appears from Scripture which implies reference to participation in the dying and rising of Christ, to the forgiveness of sins in and through Christ, to

the new birth of water and of the Spirit and to the incorporation into his Body.

c. Invocation of the Holy Spirit.

d. Renunciation of evil (possibly accompanied by exorcism).

e. Profession of faith in Christ and the affirmation of allegiance to God: Father, Son and Holy Spirit.

f. Declaration that the persons baptized have acquired a new identity as sons and daughters of God, and as members of the Church, called to be witnesses of the Gospel and to strive for the realization of the will of God in all realms of life.

It is especially the latter aspect of our rebirth that is strongly emphasized in *Confessing the One Faith*:

> "*By its strong emphasis on baptism as the sacrament for the remission of sins, the Creed exhorts us to take our baptism seriously as essentially linked to the beginning of a new life, the **decisive and fundamental change** in our life history that occurs once for all*" [11].

Infant Baptism, Adult Baptism and Confirmation

In view of the agreement between the churches on the theology and the liturgy of baptism, the differences between infant and adult baptism and the different confirmation rites also appear in a new light.

The central point in every baptism will always have to be the personal confession of faith and the preparedness to participate in the Christian community in which one is baptized. In the case of adults, the baptized person can make his own personal confession of faith and commitment.

The baptism of infants anticipates this personal confession of faith and act of commitment. In both cases, the baptized person will have to grow in the understanding of faith. For those baptized

[11] *Confessing the One Faith*, 93.

upon their own confession of faith, there is always the constant requirement of a continuing growth of personal response in faith. In the case of infants, personal confession is expected later, and Christian nurture is oriented to the eliciting of this confession.

Thus, the necessity of faith for the reception of the salvation embodied and set forth in baptism is acknowledged by all churches. Personal commitment is necessary for responsible membership in the body of Christ. Hence, the identity of adult baptism and infant baptism can only be evident if the churches insist on the necessity of the vicarious faith of the congregation as well as of the parents and sponsors. The act of faith also involves the belief that participation in the corporate life of the Body of Christ is an essential element in the salvation of each member, and that the baptized infant is initiated into this corporate life. Indiscriminate infant baptism is irresponsible and turns infant baptism into an act which can hardly be understood to be essentially the same as adult baptism. The gap between infant baptism and adult baptism is only bridged by speaking of baptism as part of a process of Christian nurture that includes:

a. the growth of a child within a supportive Christian community;

b. a personal, public confession of faith at an appropriate age, and

c. faithful discipleship throughout one's life[12].

The different understandings of chrismation and confirmation constitute a particular problem for the mutual recognition of both baptism and confirmation. Here again, much could be gained by stressing the unity of the baptismal initiation. Though initiation may be effected in two stages, the once-for-all character of baptism should neither be diminished nor destroyed. Confirmation, whether given sacramental significance or not, tends to give the impression of qualifying the uniqueness of baptism or even of repeating it. The once-for-all character of baptism must be preserved, however.

[12] Cf. M. Kinnamon, *Truth and Community*, 40-48, esp. 45.

Confirmation must not be allowed to take over certain elements which belong properly to baptism alone. For example, though in all traditions in which confirmation (chrismation) is thought of as a sacrament it is associated with the gift of the Spirit, it would be wrong to understand baptism exclusively as the sign of the forgiveness of sins, while the gift of the Spirit is exclusively connected with confirmation. As long as baptism and confirmation are administered simultaneously, there is little danger of such separation. Confirmation cannot do more than underline or, for some traditions, complete what has already been achieved in baptism.

Nevertheless, it remains extremely important to endorse the position that the baptismal event needs to be recalled, and that some provision needs to be made so that baptism can be an ever present reality. This is especially important for those who have been baptized as infants. The opportunity must be given for the appropriation of baptism by personal confession and engagement. In many churches confirmation provides this opportunity. But can this recalling and re-affirmation of baptismal vows take place on one given occasion? Is there not need for several occasions? Does not this once-for-all confirmation rather blur than underline the once-for-all character of baptism? In any case, confirmation should not take place exclusively at a fixed age, but should rather be performed when the candidate is ready for it on his or her own initiative.

The once-for-all character of baptism calls for immediate admission to the eucharist. If admission is deferred, the impression is created that incorporation into the Body of Christ has not yet fully taken place. Should baptism not be the gateway to eucharistic fellowship? Several churches have been led to admit children to the eucharist at a much earlier age than they used to do in the past. They do not regard confirmation or personal confession as the condition for admission to the eucharist. Instead, they dissociate admission from confirmation and allow it to take place at an earlier age. Although this is in the logic of emphasizing the unity of the baptismal initiation, it should not diminish the insistence on the provision for opportunities of genuine personal commitment (confirmation, confession, etc.).

New Elements in the Lima Text

With respect to the 1971 report "Baptism, Confirmation and Eucharist", which underlies the Lima text, it strikes one that, in Lima, a quite specific role is also played by three aspects of the theology of baptism which have hardly been mentioned before, namely, the symbolic character of water, the meaning of baptism for ethics and the rise of a number of questions that are closely related to the inculturation of the gospel in non-Western cultures.

With respect to the symbolic character of water the Lima text observes:

> "In the celebration of baptism the symbolic dimension of water
> should be taken seriously and not minimalized. The act of immer-
> sion can vividly express the reality that in baptism the Christian
> participates in the death, burial and resurrection of Christ" [13].

There is awareness of the fact that some African churches prac-tise baptism of the Holy Spirit without water, through the laying on of hands, while recognizing the baptism of other churches. And there is the intention to study in greater detail the relation of this baptismal practice to the one with water. Indeed, it is precisely the African churches including those who do not use water, who point out to the Western churches their inadequate understanding of the symbolic meaning of the sacraments[14]. Hence in the evaluation

---

[13] *Baptism, Eucharist and Ministry*, 6 (B.18). Cf. also the Commentary on this part of the text: "As seen in some theological traditions, the use of water, with all its positive associations with life and blessing, signifies the continuity between the old and new creation, thus revealing the significance of baptism not only for human beings but also for the whole cosmos. At the same time, the use of water represents a purification of creation, a dying to that which is negative and destruc-tive in the world: those who are baptised into the body of Christ are made partak-ers of a renewed existence".

[14] Cf. W. Eggen, "African Roads into the Theology of Earthly Realities", *Exchange* 22 (1993) 91-161 and G. van 't Spijker, "Man's Kinship with Nature: African Reflection on Creation", *Exchange* 23 (1994) 89-148. These two articles by a Roman Catholic and Protestant missiologist respectively, both temporary members of the staff of the Department of Missiology of the Interuniversity Insti-tute for Missiological and Ecumenical Research at Leiden (the Netherlands), can be considered as an Africa-oriented elaboration of my study *Schepping en Sacra-*

report on the responses of the churches to the Lima text the Faith and Order Commission under the heading "Major Issues Demanding Further Study" observes:

> *"The cosmological dimensions of the sacraments be further studied, taking into account the material elements used in the sacraments (representing creation and human labour), and the fact that the sacraments touch and are also touched by all aspects of human life. The sacraments, as instances of God's redemptive activity, have an exemplary and critical function towards the use and abuse of nature. They contribute to the transformation of the world according to God's purpose for humanity and creation, to be ultimately fulfilled at the end of ages"* [15].

As far as the ethical consequences of baptism are concerned, the Lima text quite explicitly tries to join the biblical images which speak of an exodus from bondage (I Cor.10:1-2[16]) and a liberation into a new humanity in which barriers of division whether of sex or race or social status are transcended (Gal.3:27-28 and I

---

ment, planned within the framework of a common study project on sacraments and world experience.

[15] *Baptism, Eucharist & Ministry 1982-1990*, 146. See further the report of Section I of the Seventh World Assembly of the World Council of Churches in Canberra (1991) in: M. Kinnamon (ed.), *Signs of the Spirit*, 57: "The sacraments of Christian worship use the elements of the created world to manifest the Triune God present among and in us. This sacramental Christian perspective influences our approach to the creation in general". Personally I was indirectly slightly involved in the wording of these phrases as participant at the BEM evaluation consultation in Annecy (France) and in the work of section I at the World Asssembly in Canberra. In my study *Schepping en Sacrament. Een oecumenische studie naar de reikwijdte van het sacrament als heilzaam symbool in een weerbarstige werkelijkheid*, Zoetermeer 1991, esp. 169/170 I strongly endorsed the materiality of the sacrament: "Through the language of symbols which is peculiar to every aspect of the earthly reality a whole 'world' of experiences is conveyed in the sacrament. In that sense the language of the reality in which we live is a very explicit component of the sacrament .... Thus, through the symbols of water, bread and wine the sacrament is always at the centre of creation and in this manner the sacrament takes everything that belongs to creation symbolically – using biblical images – to the bank of the river Jordan (baptism) and to the foot of the cross of Golgotha (eucharist)".

[16] I Cor.10:1-2: "You should understand, my brothers, that our ancestors were all under the pillar of cloud, and all of them passed through the Red Sea; and so they all received baptism into the fellowship of Moses in cloud and sea".

Cor.12:13[17]). In baptism we are given a new ethical orientation
which calls for more than alone personal sanctification. It will be
clear that this strong accentuation of the ethical implications of
baptism is especially directed against the practice of infant baptism, in an apparently indiscriminate way, in many large European
and North American Roman Catholic, Protestant and Orthodox
majority churches. When infant baptism is practised without any
form of Christian nurture afterwards, and without active participation in the life of the church, there is little point in speaking about
a new identity as sons and daughters of God. The reflection on the
way in which the theology of baptism should continually change
the face of the church as a new community in Christ has then been
robbed of its foundation: reborn members. And this while the
evaluation report of the responses to the Lima text precisely rec-
ommends further study on the social dimension of the sacraments:

> "Such a study should take into account St Paul's critique of dis-
> crimination and division in the community (I Cor.11). The study
> should also apply the concept and reality of the new community
> created by word and sacrament in the church both to individual
> problems like loneliness, despair and hopelessness, and also to the
> social problems of a divided humanity such as riches and poverty,
> oppression, totalitarianism, militarism, discrimination on account
> of race, sex, ethnic or religious identity" [18].

The question of inculturation concentrates in particular on
name-giving in the liturgy of baptism. There is the specific intention to pay more attention to the questions encouraged by the
socio-cultural context in which baptism takes place, since – as is
acknowledged – in some parts of the world name-giving in the
baptismal liturgy has led to confusion between baptism and cus-

---

[17] Gal.3:27-28: "Baptized into union with him, you have all put on Christ as a
garment. There is no such thing as Jew and Greek, slave and freeman, male and
female; for you are all one person in Christ Jesus" and I Cor.12:13: "For indeed
we were all brought into one body by baptism, in the one Spirit, whether we are
Jews or Greeks, whether slaves or free men, and that one Holy Spirit was poured
out for all of us to drink".
[18] *Baptism, Eucharist & Ministry 1982-1990*, 146.

toms surrounding name-giving. This confusion is especially harmful if, in cultures predominantly non-Christian, the baptized are required to assume Christian names not rooted in their own cultural tradition. In making regulations for baptism, churches should be careful to keep the emphasis on the true Christian significance of baptism and to avoid unnecessarily alienating the baptized from their local culture through the imposition of foreign names. A name which is inherited from one's original culture roots the baptized in that culture, and, at the same time, manifests the universality of baptism, incorporation into the one Church, which stretches over all the nations of the earth[19].

In the section of the Lima text on the eucharist, in which it is said that the affirmation of a common eucharistic faith does not imply uniformity in either liturgy or practice, something of these questions of inculturation can also be heard, albeit quite tentatively, in the commentary on this text fragment:

> *"Since New Testament days, the Church has attached the greatest importance to the continued use of the elements of bread and wine which Jesus used at the Last Supper. In certain parts of the world, where bread and wine are not customary or obtainable, it is now sometimes held that local food and drink serve better to anchor the eucharist in everyday life. Further study is required concerning the question of which features of the Lord's Supper were unchangeably instituted by Jesus, and which features remain within the Church's competence to decide"*[20].

Especially around the three latter aspects – the symbolic meaning of the baptismal rite, the ethical meaning of baptism and the embedding of this sacrament in non-Western cultures – a lively discussion might arise in the next few years.

In fact, the first aspect is directly related to the third aspect and the question is (again) essential, not only for non-Western, but also for Western cultures: To what extent can old Christian symbols be integrated into modern cultures with quite specific symbols of their own?

---

[19] Cf. *Baptism, Eucharist and Ministry*, 7 (Commentary on B.21).
[20] *Ibid.*, 17 (Commentary on E.28).

With regard to the second aspect, the ethical implications of baptism, what is essential is the question of the extent to which Christians succeed in deriving a credible and authentic Christian profile of behaviour from the baptismal vows, so that their communities may radiate something of the coming kingdom of God in our present cultures.

CHAPTER V

EUCHARIST

Anamnesis

Whereas baptism embodies what makes a Christian a Christian, the eucharist embodies the continuous experience of being a Christian. Even more penetratingly than in baptism, in the eucharist the memorial (anamnesis) to Christ's words and actions is kept alive. While invoking the Holy Spirit, the prospect of the coming kingdom of peace is preserved and church and world are most deeply experienced as one community in the light of God's love (agape) for the whole of his creation. It is especially these three aspects, anamnesis, epiklesis and agape – in the Lima text consistently replaced by the word communion – which have received increasing attention in ecumenical reflection on the eucharist, and which are the building blocks of the Lima text on the eucharist[1].

In the concept of anamnesis, the idea of the history of salvation becomes quite explicitly manifest. The Christian position is determined by the memory of the salvation granted in the history of Israel and the church, and by the expectation of the salvation to be unfolded in God's kingdom of peace.

In the concept of epiklesis, the realization of our inability to keep alive this memory – a memory which arouses so many

---

[1] Cf. G. Wainwright's "Historical Sketch" in: M. Thurian/G. Wainwright (eds.), *Baptism and Eucharist*, 100-110 and M. Thurian, "The Eucharistic Memorial, Sacrifice of Praise and Supplication" and J.M.R. Tillard, "The Eucharist, Gift of God" in: M. Thurian (ed.), *Ecumenical Perspectives*, 90-103, 104-118 and also 198-209 ("Provisional Draft of an Ecumenical Consensus on Eucharist" (1952) and "Second Draft on "The Eucharist in Ecumenical Thought" (1967)).

expectations – becomes clearly visible. It is only in the prayer for
the Spirit that we see concretely before our eyes the salvific significance of the body that is broken and the blood that is shed.
Not until then do we really realize how this communion connects
us with each other in love (agape).

These three accents were quite plainly laid in the report, "The
Holy Eucharist", for the Faith and Order Conference in Bristol
(1967)[2]. The Lima text elaborates on them:

> *"The eucharist is the memorial of the crucified and risen Christ,*
> *i.e. the living and effective sign of his sacrifice, accomplished once*
> *for all on the cross and still operative on behalf of all humankind.*
> *The biblical idea of memorial as applied to the eucharist refers to*
> *this present efficacy of God's work when it is celebrated by God's*
> *people in a liturgy.*
> *Christ himself with all that he has accomplished for us and for all*
> *creation (in his incarnation, servanthood, ministry, teaching, suf-*
> *fering, sacrifice, resurrection, ascension and sending of the Spirit)*
> *is present in this anamnesis, granting us communion with himself.*
> *The eucharist is also the foretaste of his parousia and of the final*
> *kingdom"* [3].

The anamnesis in which Christ acts through the joyful celebration of his Church is thus both representation and anticipation. It is
not only a calling to mind of what is past, or of its significance. It
is the Church's effective proclamation of God's mighty acts and
promises. Thus the eucharist is neither the occasion of a simple
mental recollection of Christ and his death, nor yet a repetition of
Calvary.

Here, it is already possible to read between the lines how the
Lima text takes sides in the old Rome-Reformation controversies
on the nature of the sacrifice of the mass and the nature of Christ's
real presence (presentia realis) in the elements of bread and wine.
As opposed to the Protestant suspicion that the sacrifice of Christ
on the cross is repeated in the mass, the text explicitly speaks of

---

[2] Cf. G. Gassmann (ed.), *Documentary History*, 81-88, esp. 82/83 (anamnesis and
epiklesis) and 84-86 (eucharist and agape).
[3] *Baptism, Eucharist and Ministry*, 11 (E.5 and 6).

"his sacrifice, accomplished once for all on the cross" and of "the unique sacrifice", and even explicitly expels every notion of 'repetition':

> *"What it was God's will to accomplish in the incarnation, life, death, resurrection and ascension of Christ, God does not repeat. These events are unique and can neither be repeated nor prolonged"* [4].

In this common accentuation of the unicity and unrepeatability of the sacrifice on the cross, an important Protestant objection against the Roman Catholic theology of the eucharist is removed. Any thought of Christ being again sacrificed or of the priest as a 'Christus prolongatus' has been expelled here.

Nevertheless, the accentuation of the unicity of Christ's sacrifice on the cross does not exclude the possibility of also speaking of a unicity of Christ's presence in the eucharist. Here the Lima text quite emphatically endorses an important element from Roman Catholic theology which certainly in the Reformed tradition – although not in Calvin himself – had rather receded into the background[5]. Nowhere else is he as really present as in the eucharist, as the Lima text underlines in a direct reference to Jesus:

> *"The words and acts of Christ at the institution of the eucharist stand at the heart of the celebration; the eucharistic meal is the sacrament of the body and blood of Christ, the sacrament of his*

[4] *Ibid.*, 11/12 (E.8). In the Commentary on these phrases the Lima text says (11): "It is in the light of the significance of the eucharist as intercession that references to the eucharist in Catholic theology as 'propitiatory sacrifice' may be understood. The understanding is that there is only one expiation, that of the unique sacrifice of the cross, made actual in the eucharist and presented before the Father in the intercession of Christ and of the Church for all humanity".
[5] Cf. R.M. Shelton, "A Theology of the Lord's Supper from the Perspective of the Reformed Tradition" in: D.K. McKim (ed.), *Major Themes in the Reformed Tradition*, Grand Rapids 1992, 259-270, esp. 260-264 ("The Real or True Presence of Jesus Christ"): "One cannot read Calvin, the father of Reformed Theology, without being struck, if not overwhelmed, by the prominence that the real or true presence of Jesus Christ has in his theological statements regarding the Lord's Supper"(261). See also M.E. Brinkman, *Schepping en Sacrament*, 49-52 ("Schepping en Sacrament bij Calvijn").

> *real presence. Christ fulfils in a variety of ways his promise to be always with his own even to the end of the world. But Christ's mode of presence in the eucharist is unique. Jesus said over the bread and wine of the eucharist: 'This is my body .... This is my blood'. What Christ declared is true, and his truth is fulfilled every time the eucharist is celebrated. The Church confesses Christ's real, living and active presence in the eucharist"* [6].

Two extremes are avoided in this formulation. One extreme would be to hold that bread and wine had no part in Christ's presence in the eucharist. Such a position is untenable in view of a clear witness of Scripture and an overwhelming tradition of Christianity. The other extreme would be to hold that Christ's eucharistic presence is limited to bread and wine. This position is also untenable in the light of an equally clear witness of Scripture and in the light of a centuries old Christian witness in which Christ is also held to be present there where people assemble in his name and the faithful have embraced him in their hearts (Matt. 18:20; Col.3:16; Gal.2:20 and Col.1:27[7]). It is within this universe of meaning that any ecumenical confession of Christ's presence in the eucharist must be made[8].

This *presentia realis* is closely bound up with the faith of the community within which the eucharist is celebrated. It is not something factual which might be discerned because of the objective change of bread and wine: nor, however, is it something completely individual: "While Christ's real presence in the eucharist does not depend on the faith of the individual, all agree that to discern the body and the blood of Christ, faith is required"[9].

Christians believe that by the words of Jesus and by the power of the Holy Spirit, the bread and wine of the eucharist become, in

---

[6] *Baptism, Eucharist and Ministry*, 12 (E.13).
[7] Matt.18:20: "For where two or three have met together in my name, I am there among them"; Col.1:27: "The secret is this: Christ in you, the hope of a glory to come"; Col.3:16: "Let the message of Christ dwell among you in all its richness" and Gal.2:20: "I have been crucified with Christ: the life I now live is not my life, but the life which Christ lives in me".
[8] Cf. *Baptism, Eucharist & Ministry 1982-1990*, 117.
[9] *Baptism, Eucharist and Ministry*, 12 (E.13).

a real though mysterious manner, the body and the blood of the risen Christ, i.e., of the living Christ present in all his fullness. Under the signs of bread and wine, the deepest reality is the total being of Christ who comes to us in order to feed us and transform our entire being. Although the presence of the crucified and risen Christ at the eucharist is a pneumatic presence, a presence by the power of the Holy Spirit, there is no thought here of a contrast between the 'realiter' and 'spiritualiter' character of his presence. Once again it is not either/or. Memorial (anamnesis) and real presence go hand in hand[10].

The very concept of anamnesis makes it possible to fix the presence of Christ in the eucharist not exclusively on the elements of bread and wine, but to relate them to the content of the whole celebration of word and sacrament:

> " Since the **anamnesis** of Christ is the very content of the preached Word as it is of the eucharistic meal, each reinforces the other. The celebration of the eucharist properly includes the proclamation of the Word" [11].

On the basis of the answers of the churches to the Lima text, the evaluation report eventually arrives at the following balanced formulations with respect to the relation between the preaching of the word and the administering of the sacraments:

> "Both by its meaning and function the service of word and sacrament occupies a central place in the life of the church .... In terms of liturgical structures, it may be appropriate to envisage the single service of word and sacrament as an ellipse with two foci. All churches recognize that a service of the word may have its own integrity. The question then remains of the appropriate frequency of the eucharist celebration in the narrower sense, i.e. the Lord's

---

[10] M. Kinnamon, *Truth and Community*, 42/43.

[11] *Baptism, Eucharist and Ministry*, 12 (E.12). Cf. also *Ibid.*, 10 (E.3): "The eucharist, which always includes both word and sacrament, is a proclamation and celebration of the work of God". The Bristol report, which underlies the Lima text, expresses itself here in even slightly stronger terms: "Eucharist should not be celebrated without the ministry of the Word, and the ministry of the Word points to, and is consummated in the Eucharist". Cf. G. Gassmann (ed.), *Documentary History*, 82/83.

supper or holy communion. The responses of many Protestant churches declare – sometimes with the acknowledgment of the stimulus provided by the Lima text – their acceptance in principle of a weekly, or Sunday, eucharist. The Orthodox and Roman Catholic churches, long familiar with the eucharist as the principal service of Sunday, now experience a renewal of preaching" [12].

Epiklesis

Anamnesis points to epiklesis, for it is the Spirit who makes Christ really present in the eucharist and able to be given to us in bread and wine. Being assured by Jesus' promise in the words of institution that its prayer will be answered, the Church confidently prays for the Spirit, in order that the eucharistic event may be a reality: the real presence of the crucified and risen Christ giving his life for all humanity:

> *"It is in virtue of the living word of Christ and by the power of the Holy Spirit that the bread and wine become the sacramental signs of Christ's body and blood"* [13].

The invocation of the Spirit on the elements should never be isolated from the epiklesis on the community, while an epiklesis on the community assembled for the eucharist implies a reference to bread and wine, which become the sacramental signs of Christ's body and blood. Because of the epikletic character of the whole eucharist, the epiklesis should be clearly expressed in all liturgies as the invocation of the Spirit upon the people of God and upon the whole eucharistic action, including the elements. The consecration cannot be limited to a particular moment in the liturgy. Nor is the location of the epiklesis in relation to the words of institution of decisive importance. In the early liturgies the whole 'prayer action' was thought of as bringing about the reality promised by Christ.

---

[12] *Baptism, Eucharist & Ministry 1982-1990*, 113.
[13] *Baptism, Eucharist and Ministry*, 13 (E.15).

The strongly epikletic character of the Lima text on eucharist is closely related to the trinitarian framework within which one puts the eucharist. The bond between the eucharistic celebration and the mystery of the Triune God reveals the role of the Holy Spirit as that of the One who makes the historical words of Jesus present and alive. In the 'Commentary' on these paragraphs, it is explained that this emphasis on the decisive role of the Spirit is not to spiritualize the eucharistic presence of Christ but to affirm the indissoluble union between the Son and the Spirit. This union makes it clear that the eucharist is not a magical or mechanical action but a prayer addressed to the Father, one which emphasizes the Church's utter dependence.

Agape

The Bristol report on the eucharist, in particular, emphasizes the meaning of the New Testament concept of agape. The term is missing in the Lima text, but the basic idea certainly is not[14].
Agape in early Christian usage designates a communal meal explicitly observed in the name and presence of Christ. The term reflects God's self-revealed love between God in Christ and the Church, love between Christians themselves, and love emanating from God via his believing people to and for the world in active concern and responsiveness.

---

[14] On the gradual separation of agape and eucharist the Bristol report on the eucharist observes the following: "For reasons we cannot fully know, the Agape and the Eucharist became clearly separate observances in the Church. The Agape followed its own ceremonial with emphasis on fraternal responsibility in human affairs. But the danger was always that Agapes would lose their integrity as manifestations of the basic oneness of Christians and the love revealed in Christ. It is significant that they first came under attack for so losing their integrity (I Cor.11:21-22; Jude 12 and II Peter 2:13). This loss no doubt contributed to the eventual disappearance of the Agape as a regular communal meal in the Church". Cf. G. Gassmann (ed.), *Documentary History*, 85.

Although the precise relation of the Agape to the Eucharist in earliest Christian practice is not clear[15], all communal meals mentioned in the New Testament, if not necessarily eucharistic, were surely intended to be agapeic. The term agapeic here signifies a covenantal relationship in which the members of the community both recognized their common existence in Christ and pledged to live for one another's total welfare according to, and as they were involved in, God's servant-love in Christ.

The eucharist, in the institution at the Last Supper and in subsequent celebrations, involves, as does the Agape, communal eating and drinking. Such action, especially in Hebraic and early Christian thought, implies an agapeic relationship which was meant to find expression in all the affairs of God's people.

As the Church's liturgy and structured life developed, these agapeic implications were given specific expression in connection with the Eucharist: for example, in the mutual forgiveness of sins; the kiss of peace; the bringing of gifts for the communal meal and for distribution to the poor brethren; the specific prayer for the needy and suffering; the taking of the elements of the eucharist to the sick and the imprisoned. In this agapeic realization of eucharistic fullness, the ministry of deacons and deaconesses was especially significant.

The place of such a ministry between the table and the needy properly testifies to the redeeming presence of Christ in the world. All these agapeic features of the Eucharist are directly related to Christ's own testimony. Christians themselves participate in his servanthood by virtue of their union with him. As God in Christ has entered into the human situation, so should eucharistic liturgy be near to the concrete and particular situations of men[16].

In the Lima text on eucharist the references to the meal aspects of the eucharist have been integrated into the anamnesis:

---

[15] Cf. R. Feneberg, *Christliche Passafeier und Abendmahl. Eine biblisch-hermeneutische Untersuchung der neutestamentlichen Einsetzungsberichte* (Studien zum Alten und Neuen Testament, Bd. XXVII), München 1971 and G.A.M. Rouwhorst, *De viering van de eucharistie in de vroege kerk*, Utrecht 1992.
[16] Cf. G. Gassmann (ed.), *Documentary History*, 84/85.

*"The meals which Jesus is recorded as sharing during his earthly ministry proclaim and enact the nearness of the Kingdom, of which the feeding of the multitudes is a sign. In his last meal, the fellowship of the Kingdom was connected with the imminence of Jesus' suffering. After his resurrection, the Lord made his presence known to his disciples in the breaking of the bread. Thus the eucharist continues these meals of Jesus during his earthly life and after his resurrection, always as a sign of the Kingdom. Christians see the eucharist prefigured in the Passover memorial of Israel's deliverance from the land of bondage and in the meal of the Covenant on Mount Sinai (Ex.24). It is the new paschal meal of the Church, the meal of the New Covenant, which Christ gave to his disciples as the **anamnesis** of his death and resurrection, as the anticipation of the Supper of the Lamb (Rev.19:9). Christ commanded his disciples thus to remember and encounter him in this sacramental meal, as the continuing people of God, until his return. The last meal celebrated by Jesus was a liturgical meal employing symbolic words and actions. Consequently the eucharist is a sacramental meal which by visible signs communicates to us God's love in Jesus Christ"* [17].

In this emphasizing of the background of the eucharist as a meal, the communal character of the eucharist is explicitly expressed. The sharing in one bread and the common cup, in a given place, demonstrates and effects the oneness of the sharers with Christ and with their fellow sharers in all times and places. This has ethical implications as well. The eucharistic celebration demands reconciliation and sharing among all those regarded as brothers and sisters in the one family of God and is a constant challenge in the search for appropriate relationships in social, economic and political life. All kinds of injustice, racism, separation and lack of freedom are radically challenged when we share in the body and blood of Christ[18].

---

[17] *Baptism, Eucharist and Ministry*, 10 (E.1).
[18] Cf. K.A. David, *Sacrament and Struggle: Signs and Instruments of Grace from the Downtrodden*, Geneva 1994 and Th. Wieser (ed.), *Whither Ecumenism? A Dialogue in the Transit Lounge of the Ecumenical Movement*, Geneva 1986, esp. 62-103 ("Action and Icon – Messianic Sacramentality and Sacramental Ethics").

Although the agape and eucharist became clearly separate
observances in the Church, the above-mentioned aspects of the
essentially agapeic character of the eucharist are more than worth
emphasizing today. In the light of these considerations, for example, the renewal of the diaconate office deserves serious consideration.

Thanksgiving to the Father and Meal of the Kingdom

In the accentuation of the eucharist as thanksgiving to the
Father and as the eschatological meal of the kingdom, the
Lima text very clearly breaks through the purely individual and
social contexts within which the eucharist is often understood.
The whole of creation is now, as it were, centred around the
redemption in Christ. Drawing upon the liturgy of the ancient
church, which – as was mentioned above – was close to the
Jewish meal traditions, and also upon the liturgy of especially
the Eastern-Orthodox Church, the Lima text understands the
eucharist as a proclamation and a celebration of the work of
God:

> *"It is the great thanksgiving to the Father for everything accom-
> plished in creation, redemption and sanctification, ... Thus the
> eucharist is the benediction (**berakah**) by which the Church
> expresses its thankfulness for all God's benefits.
> The eucharist is the great sacrifice of praise by which the Church
> speaks on behalf of the whole creation. For the world which God
> has reconciled is present at every eucharist: in the bread and
> wine, in the persons of the faithful, and in the prayers they offer for
> themselves and for all people"* [19].

In the Lima text this idea of offering, which consists of render-
ing back (reddere) thankfully to God what belongs to him, is not
only emphasized with respect to the elements of the eucharist, but
is also underlined with respect to each individual believer:

[19] *Ibid.*, 10 (E.3 and 4).

"In Christ we offer ourselves as a living and holy sacrifice in our daily lives (Rom.12:1; 1 Peter 2:5); this spiritual worship, acceptable to God, is nourished in the eucharist, in which we are sanctified and reconciled in love, in order to be servants of reconciliation in the world" [20].

This 'sacrifice of praise' has a pre-eminently eschatological dimension. The bread and wine, fruits of the earth and of human labour, are presented to the Father in faith and thanksgiving. The eucharist thus signifies what the world is to become: an offering and hymn of praise to the Creator, a universal communion in the body of Christ, a kingdom of justice, love and peace in the Holy Spirit.

These cosmological dimensions also become manifest in the reports of the Sixth World Assembly of the World Council of Churches in Vancouver (1983). These reports speak of a "eucharistic vision" of the whole of creation. It is characterized as follows:

*"Peace and justice, on the one hand, baptism, eucharist and ministry, on the other, have claimed our attention. They belong together. Indeed the aspect of Christian unity which has been most striking to us here in Vancouver is that of a **eucharistic vision**. Christ – the life of the world – unites heaven and earth, God and world, spiritual and secular. His body and blood, given us in the elements of bread and wine, integrate liturgy and diaconate, proclamation and acts of healing .... Our eucharistic vision thus encompasses the whole reality of Christian worship, life and witness, and tends – when truly discovered – to shed new light on Christian unity in its full richness of diversity"* [21].

This eucharistic vision of Vancouver was greatly inspired by the impressive speech of the Russian archpriest, Vitaly Borovoy, given there under the title, "Life in Unity"[22]. Borovoy's speech strongly emphasized the aspect of exhibiting the unity of cosmos

---

[20] *Ibid.*, 12 (E.10).
[21] Cf. D. Gill (ed.), *Gathered for Life: Official Report VI Assembly World Council of Churches – Vancouver, Canada 24 July – 10 August 1983*, Geneva-Grand Rapids 1983, 44/45.
[22] Cf. V. Borovoy, "Life in Unity", *The Ecumenical Review* 36 (1984) 3-10.

and liturgy, and especially of cosmos and eucharist, which is so characteristic of Eastern Orthodox spirituality. In the eucharist the unity of God and the world, lying behind and in front of us, already becomes reality in the present.

These broad cosmic relations of the eucharist in which the whole of creation is brought into relation with Christ's incarnation have receded into the background in the Western Church without, however, totally disappearing. Via the so-called elements, in particular, the relation to creation has remained constant. Irenaeus, for example, emphasizes the importance of the presence of bread and wine in the eucharist to demonstrate, against the Gnostics, the goodness of material creation and to emphasize the concreteness of Christian expectations for the future[23].

The common purpose underlying the doctrines of creation and of the sacraments is to simultaneously account for both God's transcendence and immanence. In a sense, the doctrine of the sacraments can be considered as a symbolic representation of the theology of creation. However, the doctrine of the sacraments also goes beyond this. If the doctrine of the sacraments were exclusively a symbolic representation of the doctrine of creation, then the Scylla of an exclusive soteriologicalization of the sacraments would be avoided, but one would ultimately be cast upon the Charybdis of an exclusive ontologicizing of the doctrine of the sacraments.

Nevertheless, it is extremely essential to recognize the antidocetic theme of the doctrines of both creation and the sacraments as constituting the point of departure for the possibility of a profound relation between God's transcendence and immanence. God did not consider himself too exalted to get involved with the earth in all its concreteness, materiality and corporality. The earth is allowed to be the bearer of salvation. Creation and the salvation witnessed in the sacraments are profoundly bound up with each other.

Every separation between creation and sacrament is fatal to the doctrine of creation as well as to the sacraments. The salvation

---

[23] Cf. Irenaeus, *Adversus Haereses*, IV, 18, 4, 17/18 (*PG*, 7,1027).

proclaimed in the sacraments would become docetic, and lose all contact with the day-to-day concrete world and the doctrine of creation would become cynically fatalistic, if there were no prospect of salvation. This is why, instead of a separation, we can rather expect to find paradoxal relations here which are similar to the "uncommingled" and "unchanged", "undivided" and "unseparated" of Chalcedon.

Viewed against the background of this awareness of the rather complicated, yet unsurrenderable, interconnectedness of the doctrine of creation and the doctrine of salvation, it seems unwise to quickly dismiss Borovoy's emphasis on the relation creation-sacrament as simply a specimen of Eastern-Orthodox spirituality.

The emphasis on this interconnectedness could be an impulse towards a breakthrough which could provide a perspective beyond too individualistic, soteriologically viewed doctrine of the sacraments. It would also give an impulse to go beyond a doctrine of creation based on the status quo which fails to see salvation as liberation of creation in travail. In this manner, the doctrine of the sacraments could be liberated from its individualistic fetters and the redemptive destiny of God's creation could be revealed[24].

Lima Liturgy

The enormous spread of the Lima text – already 24 reprints of the English text alone, with a total of 85,000 copies and about 31 translations – is undoubtedly closely related to the impressive character of the Lima liturgy for the eucharist, based on these texts, which was celebrated for the first time at the Sixth World Assembly of the World Council of Churches at Vancouver (1983), after the Lima text had been approved of by the World Assembly[25].

---

[24] Cf. M.E. Brinkman, "Creation and Sacrament", *Exchange* 19 (1990) 208-216.
[25] See for the text of the Lima liturgy, with a short introduction by M. Thurian, M. Thurian/G. Wainwright (eds.), *Baptism and Eucharist*, 241-255 and also M. Thurian (ed.), *Ecumenical Perspectives*, 225-246.

The Lima text itself does not contain any liturgy. However, at the end of the text fragment on the eucharist, there is an extensive enumeration of all the components that are indispensable for a liturgy of the eucharist. This enumeration may be more or less considered as a kind of test case with respect to the convergence formulated earlier in the text. The really important aspects of the convergence should now indeed return in the liturgy. The order of the various liturgical parts mentioned in the Lima text is in itself consistent, in the sense that it is in accordance with the accents laid by the text itself. In fact, however, the liturgy of the eucharist will still often be celebrated in varying sequence, and each tradition will make choices on the basis of the importance it attaches to the different components. The enumeration of the various liturgical components is, therefore, too exhaustive to really serve as a criterion for what is thought to be indispensable.

The significance of such an enumeration, however, may well be that it is now very easy for the various church traditions to find what they themselves have explicitly preserved from the Christian tradition and what they have lost. In this way the enumeration offers us the riches of the eucharistic tradition and highlights its component parts:

"– *hymns of praise;*
– *act of repentance;*
– *declaration of pardon;*
– *proclamation of the Word of God, in various forms;*
– *confession of faith (creed);*
– *intercession for the whole Church and for the world;*
– *preparation of the bread and wine;*
– *thanksgivings to the Father for the marvels of creation, redemption and sanctification (deriving from the Jewish tradition of the **berakah**);*
– *the words of Christ's institution of the sacrament according to the New Testament tradition;*
– *the **anamnesis** or memorial of the great acts of redemption, passion, death, resurrection, ascension and Pentecost, which brought the Church into being;*
– *the invocation of the Holy Spirit (**epiklesis**) on the community, and the elements of bread and wine (either before the words of*

> *institution or after the memorial, or both, or some other reference to the Holy Spirit which adequately expresses the 'epikletic' character of the eucharist);*
> - *consecration of the faithful to God;*
> - *reference to the communion of saints;*
> - *prayer for the return of the Lord and the definitive manifestation of his Kingdom;*
> - *the Amen of the whole community;*
> - *the Lord's prayer;*
> - *sign of reconciliation and peace;*
> - *the breaking of the bread;*
> - *eating and drinking in communion with Christ and with each member of the Church;*
> - *final act of praise;*
> - *blessing and sending"* [26].

The liturgy as actually celebrated at the World Assemblies in Vancouver (1983) and Canberra (1991) contained even more elements than have been mentioned here. What strikes one, for example, is that in the enumeration mentioned in the Lima text, the Kyrie Litany and the Gloria are wanting, while the ecumenical celebrations at conferences and meetings of the World Council of Churches are, to a large extent, specifically known for the impression made by the Kyrie song prayers from, for example, the circles of Eastern Orthodoxy, and the Gloria songs from Africa. That is why the real significance of the Lima liturgy can always be properly judged only on the basis of a concrete celebration of the liturgy based on the framework of the Lima liturgy. It is only in the concrete songs and prayers, in the concrete preaching of the Word, in the actual greeting of peace and in really sharing in Christ's gifts of grace that it becomes apparent what the ecumenical convergence on the eucharist really implies.

Intercommunion

In their responses to the Lima text, the churches acknowledged the large measure of convergence in their understanding of the

---

[26] *Baptism, Eucharist and Ministry*, 15/16.

eucharist. The eucharist is generally recognized as an essential manifestation of the communion we seek. The eucharist completes what is begun in baptism, and both sacraments are intimately connected with the life of the Church. As one of the section reports of the Faith and Order Conference at Santiago de Compostela clearly shows, there is a great convergence on the central aspects of the eucharist:

> "Gathered together as a reconciled and reconciling community, Christians celebrate the death and resurrection of Christ, who is present among us and with whom we are united. We proclaim the Word, offer thanksgiving to God for God's marvellous deeds, pray for the gift of the Holy Spirit and in this meal anticipate the coming of a new heaven and a new earth" [27].

In the continuing effort to reconcile the different approaches to the sacrificial character of the eucharist and the different understandings of the nature of Christ's presence, great help has been found in the incorporation into eucharistic theology of the biblical understanding of *anamnesis* and, with it, the notion of *epiklesis*. Both concepts show that what the eucharist is about is not a magic repetition of Christ's unique sacrifice, nor a purely cognitive calling to mind of an event from the past, but a real presence effected by the Spirit.

However, this growing theological convergence with regard to the eucharist, as well as in other important aspects of the Christian faith, has not yet reached a stage that allows for eucharistic sharing among the churches. This is a matter of grave concern for all Christians. There are, nevertheless, people in many churches who, out of deep conviction and on the basis of their common baptism, knowingly engage in eucharistic hospitality, both in inviting and in receiving. They derive an important argument from the role assigned in the Lima text to the Lord as host:

---

[27] *Fifth World Conference on Faith and Order*, 25. See also Th.F. Best/G. Gassmann (eds.), *On the way to Fuller Koinonia*, 248.

> *"In the celebration of the eucharist, Christ gathers, teaches and nourishes the Church. It is Christ who invites to the meal and who presides at it. He is the shepherd who leads the people of God, the prophet who announces the Word of God, the priest who celebrates the mystery of God .... The one who presides at the eucharistic celebration in the name of Christ makes clear that the rite is not the assemblies' own creation or possession; the eucharist is received as a gift from Christ living in his Church"* [28].

Many people who accept this kind of eucharistic hospitality do not lightly transgress the boundaries of their communities, but do so out of obedience to a specific understanding of the eucharist that allows it not only to be a sign of unity but also a means of grace on the road to that fuller unity which it signifies. For others, especially for the Eastern-Orthodox churches, the eucharist is and can simply be the ultimate expression of the visible unity of the Church and not only a means to that unity [29]. Full participation in the eucharist of another church is then only possible when one own's church is in full communion with the celebrating church, and full communion means here: having all the characteristics of real unity as, for example, formulated in the unity statements of New Delhi (1961); Nairobi (1975) and Canberra (1991) (see above Chapter I).

The Roman-Catholic position, acknowledging that "eucharistic communion is inseparably linked to full ecclesial communion and its visible expression" is closest to the Eastern-Orthodox position. Nevertheless, it does also acknowledge that the sacraments "are means for building them (i.e. Christian community and spiritual life) up". In addition to the priciple that the celebration of the eucharist in a concrete community should above all be "sign of the reality of its unity in faith", the Roman-Catholic position also

---

[28] *Baptism, Eucharist and Ministry*, 16 (E.29).
[29] See for the different standpoints with regard to intercommunion the report, "Beyond Intercommunion: On the Way to Communion in the Eucharist", prepared for the Louvain meeting of Faith and Order (1971). See G. Gassmann (ed.), *Documentary History*, 89-103.

applies a second principle. In this connection there is even talk of
"two basic principles, which must always be taken into account
together". The second principle is that the Roman-Catholic
Church teaches that:

> *"by baptism members of other Churches and ecclesial Communi-*
> *ties are brought into a real, even if imperfect communion, with the*
> *Catholic Church and that 'baptism, which constitutes the sacra-*
> *mental bond of unity existing among all who through it are reborn*
> *... is wholly directed toward the acquiring of fullness of life in*
> *Christ'. The Eucharist is, for the baptized, a spiritual food which*
> *enables them to overcome sin and to live the very life of Christ, to*
> *be incorporated more profoundly in Him and share more inten-*
> *sively in the whole economy of the Mystery of Christ"* [30].

It is clear that a 'baptismal ecclesiology' plays an important role
here. However, only the more individual (personal) consequences
of this ecclesiology are elaborated by way of exception. In the
light of this second principle, "in certain circumstances, by way of
exception, and under certain conditions, access to these sacraments may be permitted, or even commended, for Christians of
other Churches and ecclesial Communities". Hence, in Western
Europe and in North America intercommunion is celebrated
weekly in many monasteries, hospitals, prisons, barracks and stu-
dent parishes, although, strictly speaking, often without the necessary consent having been given.

In the case of church 'mixed marriages' – often nearly half of
the church marriages in a number of Western European countries
where the population is more or less divided between Protestants
and Roman Catholics – both marriage partners are, as a rule, officially admitted to the eucharist by the Roman Catholic Church.
However, this admittance is restricted to the marriage service.
After their wedding-day, on the basis of the most recent ecumeni-

---

[30] Cf. *Directory for the Application of Principles and Norms on Ecumenism*,
Vatican City 1993, 68 (No. 129) with references to *Unitatis Redintegratio*, Nos. 3,
8 and 22. See further, J.E. Vercruysse, "Sacramenten in oecumenisch perspectief"
in: J. Lamberts (ed.), *Hedendaagse Accenten in de Sacramentologie: Verslagboek*
van het elfde liturgiecolloquium van het Liturgische Instituut van de K.U. Leuven -
oktober 1995, Leuven-Amersfoort 1994, 135-155, esp. 150/151.

cal directory of the Roman Catholic Church, the paradoxical situation also occurs that, if the two partners should wish to go to Communion in church, they would be violating the regulations of the church[31]. Whether joy in their shared church attendance will, in the end, overcome the ill feeling about their illegal behaviour is something that will become apparent in the future. In any case, the churches are increasingly obliged to reckon with this phenomenon and respond effectively.

---

[31] *Directory*, 76: "Although the spouses in a mixed marriage share the sacraments of baptism and marriage, Eucharist sharing can only be exceptional and in each case the norms stated above concerning the admission of a non-Catholic Christian to Eucharist communion as well those concerning the participation of a Catholic in Eucharist communion in another Church, must be observed" (No. 160). See for the ecumenical situation in this respect in the Netherlands, A. Houtepen (red.), *Oecumenisch Huwelijkspastoraat. Praktijk en achtergronden*, Amersfoort-Voorburg 1982.

CHAPTER VI

MINISTRY

Ministry and Community

The Lima text on ministry beginns with the calling of the whole people of God[1]. In a broken world God calls the whole of humanity to become God's people. For this purpose God chose Israel and then spoke in a unique and decisive way in Jesus Christ. Jesus' life of service, his death and resurrection, are the foundation of a new community which is built up continually by the good news of the Gospel and the gifts of the sacraments. The Holy Spirit unites in a single body those who follow Jesus Christ and sends them as witnesses into the world. Through Christ, their hearts and minds are directed to the consummation of the Kingdom where Christ's victory will become manifest and all things made new.

The Church is called to proclaim and prefigure the Kingdom of God. It accomplishes this by announcing the Gospel to the world and by its very existence as the body of Christ. In Jesus the Kingdom of God came among us. Christ established a new access to the Father. Living in this communion with God, all members of the Church are called to confess their faith and to give account of their hope. They are to identify with the joys and sufferings of all people as they seek to witness in caring love. This mission needs

---

[1] *Baptism, Eucharist and Ministry*, 20 (M.1). Cf. for the ministry chapter, E. Lanne, "Convergence on the Ordained Ministry" and G. Wainwright, "Reconciliation in Ministry" in: M. Thurian (ed.), *Ecumenical Perspectives*, 119-128, 129-139 and 215-224 ("First Draft of an Ecumenical Agreement on Ministry" (1972)). See for a historical survey, G. Vischer, *Apostolischer Dienst: Fünfzig Jahre Diskussion über das kirchliche Amt in Glauben und Kirchenverfassung*, Frankfurt 1982.

to be carried out in varying political, social and cultural contexts. In order to fulfil this mission faithfully, the members of the Church will seek relevant forms of witness and service in each situation. In so doing they bring to the world a foretaste of the joy and glory of God's Kingdom.

By thus relating the gospel of Jesus Christ to the whole world (following the first two chapters of the dogmatic constitution on the church of Vatican II, *Lumen Gentium*) and by allowing every believer to share in the proclamation of his message, the Lima text quite deliberately beginns the section on ministry with the question of salvation. That is what the church is aiming at and the ministry is subservient to this end. An ecclesiology or a theology of ministry should, therefore, never focus primarily on the church or on the ministry, but always on the salvation intended for everybody. For the sake of promulgating that salvation church and ministry are only instruments and signs.

A real theology of ministry attempts to indicate the way in which salvation, by divine providence, may best be handed on by people. That is a question which concerns all believers and which is directly connected with baptism. Hence, one sometimes also speaks of "the baptismal basis of all Christian ministry"[2]. By our baptism we are all challenged to be witnesses to Jesus Christ and his saving work. Being ordained to a special ministry therefore always expresses, in the first place, the will to be a real witness of God's salvation for humankind. That means the acceptance of the calling to be a real minister, a real servant of the people of God[3]. Hence, the first question with regard to the place and the form of ordained ministry is: How, according to the will of God and under the guidance of the Holy Spirit, is the life of the Church to be

---

[2] Cf. *Fifth World Conference on Faith and Order*, 26. See also Th.F. Best/G. Gassmann (eds.), *On the way to Fuller Koinonia*, 249.

[3] Cf. Y. Congar, "La Hiérarchie comme service selon le Nouveau Testament et les documents de la tradition" and "Quelques expressions traditionelles du service chrétien" in: Y. Congar/B.-D. Dupuy (eds.), *L'épiscopat et l'église universelle* (Unam Sanctam 39), Paris 1962, 69-99 and 101-132.

understood and ordered, so that the Gospel may be spread and the community built up in love? Only within the framework of this question, can the role of the ministry in the church be rightly explained.

In the second place, the charismatic character of the ministry has to be stressed. The word charism denotes the gifts bestowed by the Holy Spirit on any member of the body of Christ for the building up of the community and the fulfilment of its calling. The community which lives in the power of the Spirit will be characterized by a variety of charisms. The spirit is the giver of diverse gifts which enrich the life of the community. They may be gifts of communicating the Gospel in word and deed, gifts of healing, gifts of praying, gifts of guiding and following, gifts of inspiration and vision. All members of the church are called to discover, with the help of the community, the gifts they have received and to use them for the building up of the Church and for the service of the world to which the Church is sent.

In order to enhance their effectiveness, the community will publicly recognize certain of these charisms. While some serve permanent needs in the life of the community, others will be temporary. The ordained ministry, which is itself a charism, must not become a hindrance to the variety of these charisms. On the contrary, it is intended to help the community to discover the gifts bestowed on it by the Holy Spirit and to equip members of the body to serve in a variety of ways.

The Lima text is frequently reproached for being too high-church in as much as it takes the episcopal structure of ministry as its starting point and minimalizes the spontaneously emerging prophetic ministry[4]. In spite of this, however, the Lima document is quite explicitly interested in the new forms of ministry which the Holy Spirit is completely at liberty to employ:

---

[4] Cf. on the role of the gift of prophecy in the church, G. Vandervelde, "The Gift of Prophecy and the Prophetic Church" in: G. Vandervelde (ed.), *The Holy Spirit: Renewing and Empowering Presence*, Winfield 1989, 93-118.

> *"In the history of the Church there have been times when the truth
> of the Gospel could only be preserved through prophetic and
> charismatic leaders. Often new impulses could find their way into
> the life of the Church only in unusual ways. At times reforms
> required a special ministry. The ordained ministry and the whole
> community will need to be attentive to the challenge of such spe-
> cial ministries"* [5].

Following upon this crucial point, a third element must be
recalled. As the Louvain report (1971) on ordained ministry
stressed, certain individuals have been called and set apart to take
a decisive role in the building up of the Church. The New Testament does report a setting apart to special ministry, when distinctions of service were made. Throughout the Bible, the concept of
God's selectivity clearly emerges. There is – to quote literally the
Louvain report – a 'scandal' of particularity:

> *"God called particular people for particular tasks and set them
> apart to serve the fellowship in distinct ways. Isreal's history, its
> ever deepening awareness of having been selected by God for par-
> ticular service, the selection of prophets, priests and kings by God,
> the Incarnation itself, witness to selectivity and election. God had
> commonly called and employed individuals and groups to serve
> him in unique fashion"* [6].

The selection of apostles continued this tradition, and opened
the door to the conception of a ministry that was called and set-
apart. Against this background the existence of a ministry set apart
is fully consistent with God's *modus operandi* in calling, sending
and empowering individuals for special responsibilities. It may be
said that the Church, in ordaining new persons to ministry in
Christ's name, is attempting to follow the mission of the apostles
and remain faithful to their teaching[7]. Ordination, as an act, attests
the binding of the Church to the historical Jesus and the historical

---

[5] *Baptism, Eucharist and Ministry*, 28 (M.33).
[6] G. Gassmann (ed.), *Documentary History*, 116-136, esp. 119.
[7] Cf. J. Colson, "Le ministère apostolique dans la littérature chrétienne primitive:
apôtres et épiscopes, 'sanctificateurs des nations'" in: Y. Congar/ B.-D. Dupuy
(eds.), *L'épiscopat et l'église universelle*, 135-169.

Revelation, while, at the same time, recalling the Risen Lord, who is the true Ordainer who bestows the gift. In ordaining, the Church attempts to provide for the faithful proclamation of the Gospel and humble service in Christ's name. Ministers fulfilling such a particular ministry are ambassadors for Christ, God making His appeal through them (II Cor.5:20)[8]. Because Jesus came as one who serves (Mark 10:45 and Luke 22:27), to be set apart means to be consecrated to service.

Since ordination is essentially a setting apart with prayer for the gift of the Holy Spirit, the authority of the ordained ministry is not to be understood as the possession of the ordained person, but as a gift for the continuing edification of the body in and for which the minister has been ordained. Therefore, ministers are bound to the faithful in interdependence and reciprocity. Only when they seek the response and acknowledgement of the community can their authority be protected from the distortions of isolation and domination, although, in the strict sense of the word, their authority cannot be reduced to total dependence on the common opinion of the community. The *vocatio* of the community has to be an important aspect of the ordination rite of each church and every minister always has to seek the *consensus fidelium*. Nevertheless, his authority lies ultimately in his responsibility to express the will of God in the way Christ himself revealed God's authority to the world.

In the fourth place there is an increasing awareness of the complex character of the patterns of ministry within the New

---

[8] G. Gassmann (ed.), *Documentary History*, 120. Cf. also *Baptism, Eucharist and Ministry*, 21 where there is a reference to the scheme, especially well-known in Calvinist Protestantism, of the threefold ministry of Jesus Christ as prophet, teacher and pastor: "As heralds and ambassadors, ordained ministers are representatives of Jesus Christ to the community, and proclaim his message of reconciliation. As leaders and teachers they call the community to submit to the authority of Jesus Christ, the teacher and prophet, in whom law and prophets were fulfilled. As pastors, under Jesus Christ the chief shepherd, they assemble and guide the dispersed people of God, in anticipation of the coming Kingdom". See further also, O. Perler, "L'évêque, représentant du Christ, selon les documents des premiers siècles" in: Y. Congar (ed.), *L'épiscopat et l'église universelle*, 31-66.

Testament[9]. Therefore, it is not possible to ground *one* conception of Church order in the New Testament to the exclusion of others. It appears that, in New Testament times, differing forms coexisted and differing forms developed simultaneously in various geographical areas[10]. Hence, the Lima text concludes, the New Testament does not describe a single pattern of ministry which might serve as a blue-print or continuing norm for all future ministry in the Church.

Forms and Functions of Ministry

Although there is no single New Testament pattern, although the Spirit has frequently led the Church to adapt its ministries to contextual needs, and although other forms of ordained ministry have been blessed with the gifts of the Holy Spirit, nevertheless – so the Lima text states –:

> *"the threefold ministry of bishop, presbyter and deacon may serve today as an expression of the unity we seek and also as a means for achieving it. Historically, it is true to say, the threefold ministry became the generally accepted pattern in the Church of the early centuries and is still retained today by many churches"* [11].

This, however, by no means implies that the history of the early church presents us with a completely crystallized structure. Neither does it imply that any single church has preserved the most ideal structure of ministry. What it does imply is that there is ecu-

---

[9] Cf. for example P. Minear, *Images of the Church in the New Testament*, Philadelphia 1960; J. Dunn, *Unity and Diversity in the New Testament*, London 1977; E. Schillebeeckx, *Ministry: Leadership in the Community of Jesus Christ*, New York 1981 and K. Kertelge (Hrsg.), *Das Kirchliche Amt im Neuen Testament* (Wege der Forschung, Bd.CDXXXIX), Darmstadt 1977.

[10] Cf. H. Marot, "Unité de l'église et diversité géographique aux premiers siècles" and C. Vogel, "Unité de l'église et pluralité des formes historiques d'organisation ecclésiastique, du IIIe au Ve siècle" in: Y. Congar/B.-D. Dupuy (eds.), *L'épiscopat et l'église universelle*, 565-590 and 591-636.

[11] *Baptism, Eucharist and Ministry*, 24 (M.19).

menical agreement on the fact that there are certain functions of ministry which are given and which must be maintained in some way by the Church in every generation, and that the function of episkope (oversight), in particular – next to faithful preaching, administration of sacraments and service to humanity – belongs to these characteristics of the church of all times and of all places[12].

It is not at all clear how these functions crystallized precisely during the first centuries. At the very most a certain basic pattern may be outlined which the Lima text summarizes as follows: "In the earliest instances, where threefold ministry is mentioned, the reference is to the local eucharistic community. The bishop was the leader of the community. He was ordained and installed to proclaim the Word and preside over the celebration of the eucharist. He was surrounded by a college of presbyters and by deacons who assisted in his tasks. In this context the bishop's ministry was a focus of unity within the whole community. Soon, however, the functions were modified. Bishops began increasingly to exercise *episkope* over several local communities at the same time. In the first generation, apostles had exercised *episkope* in the wider Church. Later Timothy and Titus are recorded to have fulfilled a function of *episkope* in a given area. Later again this apostolic task is carried out in a new way by bishops. They provide a focus for unity in life and witness within areas comprising several eucharistic communities. As a consequence, presbyters become the leaders of the local eucharistic community, and as assistants of the bishops, deacons receive responsibilities in the larger area"[13].

Regardless of the precise way in which this development of the ministries took place – here the Commentary on the text is remark-

---

[12] This is the view expressed in the Memorandum of a Faith and Order consultation on "Episkope and episcopate in the ecumenical debate". See *Episkope and Episcopate in Ecumenical Perspective* (Faith and Order Paper No. 102), Geneva 1980, 2: "Episkope (overseeing, supervision) is essential for the life of the Church. No Church can live without the exercise of some kind of *episkope*". Cf. also A. van Eijk, "Episcope, episcopaat en de locale kerk" in: A. Houtepen (red.), *De verscheidenheid verzoend? Actuele thema's uit het gesprek Rome-Reformatie*, Leiden-Utrecht 1989, 165-186.

[13] Cf. *Baptism, Eucharist and Ministry*, 24 (M.20 and 21).

ably more reserved than the text itself![14] – and regardless of their names, the purpose of all these ministries was clear: to proclaim the Word of God, to transmit and safeguard the original content of the Gospel, to feed and strengthen the faith, discipline and service of the Christian communities, and to protect and foster unity within and among them. These have been the constant duties of ministry throughout the developments and crises of Christian history.

With regard to the present concrete form of the threefold ministry in the various church traditions, the Lima text does not refrain from making a number of critical observations. On the basis of the ecumenical commonly shared conviction that the ordained ministry should be exercised in a personal, collegial and communal way[15], it is asserted that the threefold pattern evidently

---

[14] *Baptism, Eucharist and Ministry*, 25 (Commentary on M.21): "The earliest Church knew both the travelling ministry of such missionaries as Paul and the local ministry of leadership in places where the Gospel was received. At local level, organizational patterns appear to have varied according to circumstances. The Acts of the Apostles mention for Jerusalem the Twelve and the Seven, and later James and the elders; and for Antioch, prophets and teachers (Acts 6:1-6; 15:13-22; 13:1). The letters to Corinth speak of apostles, prophets and teachers (I Cor.12:28); so, too, does the letter to the Romans, which also speaks of deacons or assistants (Rom.16:1). In Philippi, the secular terms episkopoi and diakonoi were together used for Christian ministers (Phil.1:1). Several of these ministries are ascribed to both women and men. While some were appointed by the laying on of hands, there is no indication of this procedure in other cases".

With regard to the presidency at the eucharist, the Louvain report on "Ordained Ministry" was also a little more reserved than the Lima text: "There is growing agreement that it is impossible to demonstrate from the New Testament that the only minister of the Lord's Supper was an ordained person. There is no clear biblical evidence that the Twelve were the exclusive ministers of the eucharist in New Testament times or that they appointed the only persons who presided at the eucharist. On the other hand, it may be noted that neither is there evidence that *all* Christians were eligible ministers of the eucharist. While in the local churches, founded by apostles like Paul, there were leaders or persons in authority, very little is said about how such men were appointed and nothing about their presiding at the eucharist". Cf. G. Gassmann (ed.), *Documentary History*, 132.

[15] See especially for this strong emphasis on the communal, collegial and personal dimension of ministry the report of the discussions within the influential French ecumenical Groupe des Dombes, *Le ministère de communion dans l'Église universelle*, Paris 1986, 89-105.

stands in need of reform. In some churches the collegial dimension of leadership in the community has suffered diminution and in others the function of deacons has been reduced to an assistant role in the celebration of the liturgy. They have ceased to fulfil any function with regard to the diaconal witness of the Church. In general, the relation of the presbyterate to the episcopal ministry has been discussed throughout centuries, and the degree of the presbyter's participation in the episcopal ministry is still, for many, an unresolved question of far-reaching ecumenical importance[16].

In spite of this unsolved ecumenical question of the exact relation between bishop and presbyter and the differences in the interpretation of the task of deacon, the Lima text nevertheless makes an attempt to describe their different functions. Bishops preach the Word, preside at the sacraments, and administer discipline in such a way as to be representative pastoral ministers of oversight, continuity and unity in the Church. They have pastoral oversight of the area to which they are called. Presbyters serve as pastoral ministers of Word and sacraments in a local eucharistic community. They are preachers and teachers of the faith, exercise pastoral care, and bear responsibility for the discipline of the congregation. Deacons represent to the Church its calling as servant in the world. By struggling in Christ's name with the myriad needs of societies and persons, deacons exemplify the interdependence of worship and service in the Church's life. They exercise a ministry of love within the community.

The ecumenical discussions about these three, as such undisputed, functions are in fact about the precise relation between local and supra-local church authority and about the relation between worship and service. We shall return to the latter relation in the chapter on church and kingdom. The discussion of the question of the relation between local and supra-local authority further

[16] Cf. Y. M.-J. Congar, "Faits, problèmes et réflexions à propos du pouvoir d'ordre et des rapports entre le presbytérat et l'épiscopat" in: Y.M.-J. Congar (ed.), *Sainte Église. Études et approches ecclésiologiques* (Unam Sanctam 41), Paris 1963, 275-302.

crystallizes in a great many fields. We shall indicate briefly three
of these fields, namely, that of the apostolic succession, of papal
authority and of the ordination of women[17].

Apostolic Succession

It was already pointed out in chapter I that the Lima text uses a
definition which is strongly determined as to content, and which
subsequently also largely determines the nature of the apostolic
succession:

> *"Apostolic tradition in the Church means continuity in the perma-
> nent characteristics of the Church of the apostles: witness to the
> apostolic faith, proclamation and fresh interpretation of the
> Gospel, celebration of baptism and the eucharist, the transmission
> of ministerial responsibilities, communion in prayer, love, joy and
> suffering, service to the sick and the needy, unity among the local
> churches and sharing the gifts which the Lord has given to
> each"* [18].

In the light of this understanding of the apostolic tradition as
regards its content, it is possible for the Lima text to say that the
primary manifestation of apostolic succession is to be found in the
apostolic tradition of the Church as a whole. The succession is an
expression of the permanence and, therefore, of the continuity of
Christ's own mission in which the Church participates[19]. The
gospel of Christ persisted in the history of the church in a great
many different ways. The succession of bishops has also played an
important role in this, although not an exclusive one:

[17] See for these and other points of discussion with regard to the ministry text
especially, M. Gosker, *Het kerkelijk ambt in het Limadocument. Een hermeneutische doorlichting en een kritische evaluatie van de Lima-Ambtstekst*, Utrecht-Leiden 1990, 71-157.
[18] *Baptism, Eucharist and Ministry*, 28 (M.34).
[19] Cf. also Y.J.-M. Congar, "Apostolicité" in: Idem, *Sainte Église: Études et
approches ecclésiologiques*, Paris 1963, 181-185, esp. 184: "L'apostolicité est
l'ensemble des caractères de *continuité sans défaillance jusqu'aux Apôtres,* aux-
quels on peut reconnaître, parmi d'autres corps religieux, la véritable Église".

> *"Under the particular historical circumstances of the growing
> Church in the early centuries, the succession of bishops became
> one of the ways, together with the transmission of the Gospel and
> the life of the community, in which the apostolic tradition of the
> Church was expressed"* [20].

In churches which practise the succession through the episcopate, it
is increasingly recognized – so the Lima text stresses[21] – that a continuity in apostolic faith, worship and mission has been preserved in
churches which have not retained the form of historical episcopate.
This recognition finds additional support in the fact that the reality and
function of the episcopal ministry have been preserved in many of
these churches, with or without the title 'bishop'. Ordination, for
example, is always performed in them by persons in whom the Church
recognizes the authority to transmit the ministerial commission.

The Primacy of the Bishop of Rome

The above-mentioned recognition from the side of the churches
with a historical episcopate helped the churches without a historical
episcopate to become aware of the fact that personal forms of
episkope are part of the common inheritance of the Church, even
though the tendency to identify this with the personal ministry of
bishops and, in particular, with the historical episcopate, is evidently
stronger in one than in the other. What was still impossible in the
Lima text, however, does appear to be already possible in Santiago de
Compostela ten years later: under the heading of *episcope* the question of the primacy of the bishop of Rome can now also become a
subject of discussion. In one of the section reports of the World Conference in Santiago it is explicitly concluded that "there is a growing
convergence amongst the churches regarding the need for a ministry
of oversight (*episkope*) at all levels in the life of the Church"[22].

[20] *Baptism, Eucharist and Ministry*, 29 (M.36).
[21] *Baptism, Eucharist and Ministry*, 29 (M.37).
[22] *Fifth World Conference on Faith and Order*, 27. See also Th.F. Best/G.
Gassmann (eds.), *On the way to Fuller Koinonia*, 250.

No doubt, the rapprochement between the Lutheran Church –
the church which in the past declared itself most strongly against
the bishop of Rome ("Antichrist!") – and the Roman Catholic
Church with respect to the acknowledgement of a universal ministry of oversight plays an important part here. The German
Lutheran-Roman Catholic dialogue on "The Condemnations of
the Reformation Era" contains a very explicit reference to this
rapprochement. The reference is, in particular, to the so-called
Malta report (1972) and the report on "Ministry in the Church"
(1981).

With regard to papal primacy, it is stated in the Malta report,
that during the discussions in the dialogue commission,
"Catholics pointed to the beginning of this doctrine in the
biblical witness concerning the special position of Peter and also
to the differences in the understanding of primacy in the first
and second millennia. By its doctrine of episcopal collegiality,
the Second Vatican Council placed the primacy in a new
interpretive framework and thereby avoided a widespread
onesided and isolated way of understanding it. The primacy of
jurisdiction must be understood as ministerial service to the
community and as bond of the unity of the church. This service
of unity is, above all, a service of unity in faith. The office of
the papacy also includes the task of caring for legitimate
diversity among local churches. The concrete shape of this
office may vary greatly in accordance with changing historical
conditions.

It was recognized on the Lutheran side that no local church
should exist in isolation since it is a manifestation of the universal
church. In this sense the importance of a ministerial service of the
communion of churches was acknowledged and, at the same time,
reference was made to the problem raised for Lutherans by their
lack of such an effective service of unity. The office of the papacy
as a visible sign of the unity of the churches was therefore not
excluded insofar as it is subordinated to the primacy of the gospel
by theological reinterpretation and practical restructuring. The
question, however, which remains controversial between Catholics

and Lutherans is whether the primacy of the pope is necessary for the church, or whether it represents only a fundamentally possible function"[23].

Ordination of Women

Against the background of the need of a deeper understanding of the comprehensiveness of ministry, which reflects the interdependence of men and women, the Lima text concludes that the churches draw different conclusions as to the admission of women to the ordained ministry. An increasing number of churches have decided that there is no biblical or theological reason against

---

[23] Cf. K. Lehmann/W. Pannenberg (eds.), *The Condemnations of the Reformation Era*, 159. See for the text of the so-called Malta report, H. Meyer/L. Vischer (eds.), *Growth in Agreement: Reports and Agreed Statements of Ecumenical Conversations on a World Level* (Faith and Order Paper No. 108), New York-Geneva 1984, 168-214, esp. 184 (No. 66). See also the text of the report on "The ministry in the Church" *Growth in Agreement*, 248-275, esp. 270/271 (No. 73): "While the traditional controversies have not yet been completely settled, it can nevertheless be said that Lutheran theologians today are among those who look not only to a future council or to the responsibility of theology, but also to a special Petrine office, when it is a question of service to the unity of the church at the universal level. Much remains theologically open here, especially the question as to how this universal ministry in the service of truth and unity can be exercised, whether by a general council, or by a group, or by an individual bishop respected by all Christians. But in various dialogues, the *possibility* begins to emerge that the Petrine office of the Bishop of Rome also need not be excluded by Lutherans as a visible sign of the unity of the church as a whole, insofar" etc. (quotation of the Malta report follows here). See further W. Klausnitzer, *Das Papstamt im Disput zwischen Lutheranern und Katholiken: Schwerpunkte von der Reformation bis zur Gegenwart* (Innsbrucker theologische Studien, Bd.20), Innsbruck-Wien 1987 and for the Anglican-Roman Catholic dialogue, *Growth in Agreement*, 62-129, esp. 96-98; 104/105 and 106-117. See also the results of the Protestant-Roman Catholic dialogue in France in the publication of the Groupe des Dombes, *Le ministère de communion dans l'Église universelle*, Paris 1986, esp. 83-88; 96-98 and 101-103 and the results of the Roman Catholic-Orthodox dialogue in France in the publication of the mixed commission edited by Jérémie and Quélen, *La Primauté Romaine dans la Communion des Églises*, Paris 1991, esp. 113-125. Cf. also J.M.R. Tillard, *L'évêque de Rome*, Paris 1982 and A. Houtepen, *De Petrusdienst van de bisschop van Rome*, Amersfoort 1985.

ordaining women, and many of them have subsequently proceeded to do so[24]. It rests for them on the deeply held theological conviction that the ordained ministry of the Church "lacks fullness"[25] when it is limited to one sex. Those churches which do not practise the ordination of women consider that the force of nineteen centuries of tradition against the ordination of women must not be set aside. They believe that there are theological issues concerning the nature of humanity and concerning Christology which lie at the heart of their convictions and understandings of the role of women in the Church[26].

The ordination of women has been especially seriously studied within the Faith and Order study project, "The Unity of the Church and the Unity of Mankind", begun in Louvain (1971). The fact that the issues of the community of women and men affect every human society, across all the diversities of nation, race and political structure, makes them a testing ground for the Christian claim to have received a truth in Christ which illuminates all human experience. The church, as mystery and prophetic sign, is called to show in a particular way how women and men are created in God's image and likeness. Hence, the study document, *Church and World*, although acknowledging that it is very difficult even to formulate questions without prejudging the answers from one point of view or another, poses the following, strongly hermeneutically focused questions:

> *"– Are the Pauline passages [on the role of women in the church] so conditioned by their specific cultural context (the Jewish-Hellenistic structure of the first century) that they no longer apply in the different culture(s) of later times?*
> *– If the passages do apply universally, do they reflect an order of creation instituted by God which continues to preclude the ordination of women to priestly ministry? Or are they a time-conditioned*

---

[24] *Baptism, Eucharist and Ministry*, 24 (M.18).
[25] *Ibid.*, 25 (Commentary on M.18). This expression seems to be a deliberate allusion to the famous phrase in the *Decree on Ecumenism* (no.22) of Vatican II with regard to the "separated churches in the West" which "lack the fullness of unity with us which flows from baptism".
[26] *Baptism, Eucharist and Ministry*, 24/25 (Commentary on M.18).

response to distortions of the order of creation caused by human sinfulness, and therefore no longer applicable in the light of what we have come to recognize as the fundamental equality of women and men in Christ?

– *If the latter is the case, has the new order of redemption inaugurated by Jesus Christ overcome these consequences of human sinfulness so as to open all ministries in the church to both men and women?*

– *In addressing these hermeneutical issues how should one relate Tradition, and its expression of the equality of women and men in terms of their equal access to salvation in Christ, to distinctions of appropriate function in the ministries of the church?*

– *How are the various particularities of Jesus' humanity – his being born a Jew, at a particular time, speaking (a) particular language(s), being male – related to the representation of the risen Christ in the life of the church? What is the significance for Christians today of the traditional emphasis on the last of these factors, namely that Jesus was male?*[27]

---

[27] *Church and World: The Unity of the Church and the Renewal of Human Community* (Faith and Order Paper No 151), Geneva 1990, 61/62. See further S. Herzel, *A Voice for Women: The Women's Department of the World Council of Churches*, Geneva 1981, esp. 65-71; C.F. Parvey (ed.), *Ordination of Women in Ecumenical Perspective: Workbook for the Church's Future* (Faith and Order Paper No. 105), Geneva 1980, esp. 54-64; Idem (ed.), *The Community of Women and Men in the Church: The Sheffield Report*, Geneva 1983, esp. 81-93; B. Thompson, *A Chance to Change: Women and Men in the Church*, Geneva 1982, esp. 82-89; M. Gosker, *Het Kerkelijk Ambt in het Limadocument*, esp. 123-131 and Th.F. Best (ed.), *Beyond Unity-in-Tension: Unity, Renewal and the Community of Women and Men* (Faith and Order Paper No.138), Geneva 1988 with, among others, contributions by C.F. Parvey. J. Crawford and E. Schüssler Fiorenza.

CHAPTER VII

CHURCH AND KINGDOM

Costly Unity

The World Council of Churches is regarded by some primarily as the organizer of an endless series of meetings at which arcane points of theology are tediously examined in slow motion, while the curtains are closed to prevent the problems of the world outside from intruding on the reading of papers. Others see the World Council as a political agency so preoccupied with the problems of the world that its only interest in religion is to use a few passages from the Bible to prooftext its radical activities[1].

This cleft between ecumenical forces committed to visible church unity and those focused on witness, service and moral struggle goes deep and exposes a history of differences which runs the length of the modern ecumenical movement. This twofold image has accompanied the World Council from its origin and is often interpreted as the classic opposition between the World Council departments Faith and Order and Church and Society. Yet this image is a caricature. The history of the World Council shows quite plainly that there have been continuous attempts to bridge this gap, one of the most successful attempts in this regard being the document *Costly Unity,* which appeared just before the Fifth World Conference on Faith and Order. In this document there is mention of the "essential interconnectedness" of the search for the visible unity of the church and the quest for justice, peace, and caring for creation. The intrinsic interconnectedness of unity and

---

[1] Cf. J. Forest, "Seeking 'costly unity': Bridging the gap", *One World* (1993) no.185, 7-8.

service is illustrated by means of the contrast between 'cheap' unity and 'costly' unity[2]:

> "*Cheap unity avoids morally contested issues because they would disturb the unity of the church. Costly unity is dicovering the churches' unity as a gift of pursuing justice and peace. It is often acquired at a price .... Costly unity is precisely to transcend loyalty to blood and soil, nation and ethnic or class heritage in the name of the God who is one and whose creation is one. It is the unity of the church accomplished on the way of the cross, paid for by the life of Christ and the lives of the martyrs, whose witness inevitably included moral witness. This is unity which, by God's grace, breaks down dividing walls so that we might be reconciled to God and one another .... Its enemy is cheap unity – forgiveness without repentance, baptism without discipleship, life without daily dying and rising in a household of faith (oikos) that is to be the visible sign of God's desire for the whole inhabited earth (the* **oikoumene**)"[3].

In the document, *Costly Unity*, this 'costly' unity is directly related to the moral meaning of the sacraments themselves:

> "*Baptism, for example, is at the heart of the church insofar as the baptized become the effective witness – martyr – to gospel values in the world. Questions of faith and moral and social questions are inseparable from the act of Christian witness that baptism mandates. Eucharist as a sacrament of communion, to cite a second example, is real food for a scattered people in their moral struggle, to heal the brokenness of human being and community. The church sees both in inner unity and solidarity with others as expressions of sharing the bread of life*"[4].

The participants in the consultation on 'Costly Unity' were very well aware of the fact that, within Christianity, widely differing answers are given to the question of the relation church-world. They describe five of these in broad outline:

1. The state of the world means that this is the end of history, that the Second Coming is rapidly approaching, and that, therefore, the primary task is to convert and baptize.

[2] Cf. Bonhoeffer's distinction between 'cheap' and 'costly' grace in, D. Bonhoeffer, *The Cost of Discipleship*, London 1959.
[3] Cf. *Costly Unity*, 88.
[4] *Costly Unity*, 89.

2. The world has always been this way, the poor will be always with us, there will be wars and rumours of wars. The best response of the churches is contemplative withdrawal and prayer for the world.

3. The church must offer an example of an alternative society that models itself on the values of the Kingdom of God.

4. In light of the situation in the world, the church needs to take a leading role, even giving direction to initiatives for justice and peace.

5. The church has to enter into the struggles of the people, not leading the process but sharing in it.

It will have become clear from what has been quoted above about the linking of sacrament and life, that the document *Costly Unity*, endorses especially the latter viewpoint. There is an attempt to indicate modestly, not imperialistically, what it means for the church to be 'a sign and instrument of the unity of the whole of humanity' – an expression employed in *Lumen Gentium*, No.1 of Vatican II, and adopted by the World Council of Churches at the Fourth Assembly at Uppsala in 1986[5].

Unity of the Church – Unity of Mankind

From the early seventies onwards, especially within the study project 'Unity of the Church – Unity of Mankind'[6], Faith and

---

[5] See for a really modest formulation of this claim the report of section I on "The Holy Spirit and the Catholicity of the Church", No. 20 in N. Goodall (ed.), *The Uppsala Report 1968*, 17: "The Church is bold in speaking of itself as the sign of the coming unity of mankind. However well founded the claim, the world hears it sceptically, and points to 'secular catholicities' of its own. For secular society has produced instruments of conciliation and unification which often seem more effective than the Church itself. To the outsider, the churches often seem remote and irrelevant, and busy to the point of tediousness with their own concerns. The churches need a new openness to the world in its aspirations, its achievements, its restlessness and its despair".

[6] See for the background of this project, G. Müller-Fahrenholz, *Unity in Today's World: The Faith and Order Studies on 'Unity of the Church – Unity of*

Order has looked for a point of integration between ecclesiology and service to the world and has considered this point of integration as being contained in the twofoldness of church and kingdom of God[7]. In the study document, *Church and World*, the relation Church-Kingdom is essentially summarized in three central points:

1. The Church is called to be in all aspects oriented towards the final coming of the Kingdom of which it is already a foretaste, especially in the Lord's Supper, which is the communion of Christ's eschatological meal with his people. The Church anticipates the yet greater blessings which God has in store and which surpass present human experience. That is why the Church yearns and prays so fervently: "Your kingdom come" (Matt.6:10; Luke 11:2), "Maranatha", "Our Lord, come!" (I Cor.16:22), "And the Spirit and the bride say, 'Come'" (Rev. 22:17).

2. Endowed with the gifts of the Holy Spirit and continually strengthened by Christ's word and sacrament, the Church is sent by God to witness to, and proclaim the Kingdom in and for, this broken world through word and deed, life and suffering, even suffering unto death. In this mission the Church is the new community of those willing to serve the Kingdom for the glory of God and the good of humanity. To the degree to which this happens the Church is an effective sign, an instrument of God's mission in this aeon.

3. In all this the Church participates in the paradoxes and dynamics of the Kingdom within history. It, too, is a net with good

---

Humankind (Faith and Order Paper No. 88), Geneva 1978, 27: "The concept of the 'unity of mankind' was not a product of the '60s, but was already in use in the ecumenical movement prior to the Second World War .... The ecumenical discussion always presupposed some sort of unity and solidarity of humankind .... Again and again the ecumenical conferences seek to perceive within the opportunities and sufferings, challenges and dangers of the world situation at any given moment, not only the possible questions put to the Church, but also and especially, God's call and claim .... In this sense, ecumenical theology has always been *contextual theology*, and necessarily so".

[7] See for this study project, G. Gassmann (ed.), *Documentary History*, 25-29 and 137-160.

and bad fish, a field of wheat and tares. It is a community of sinners and at the same time justified, a beginning not an end, always
endangered from within as from without, but preserved at the
same time by the grace of God in an unendingly renewing feast of
Pentecost[8].

Church as Prophetic Sign

In the perspective of the kingdom of God, Church and world
appear in their fundamental, or rather eschatological togetherness.
This is no undifferentiated, monolithic unity. It is no premature
amalgamation and confusion between Church and world. There is
a legitimate concern for the inalienable identity of the Church. The
Church is not the world and the structures of this world, though
being the realm of God's action and of the Church's mission, do
not, as such, become Church. Therefore, there is no point in speaking of the world as the "latent Church" (Tillich)[9]. The Kingdom
of God is a gift; its full realisation is the very work of God. As
partakers of the trinitarian life of God, however, the members of
the Church are called to be fellow-workers with God (I Cor.3:9)
for the implementation of the values of the Kingdom in the
world[10].

It can be said that the concept of 'sign' offers the best interpretative key to the relation between the unity of the Church and the
unity of humanity. It safeguards the self-critical reference to the
Church's dependence on its Lord. The sign itself is nothing with-

[8] *Church and World*, 23/24. Cf. also G. Limouris (ed.), *Church Kingdom World:
The Church as Mystery and Prophetic Sign* (Faith and Order Paper No. 130),
Geneva 1986, esp. 167/168 and *Fifth World Conference on Faith and Order*, 35-
37 (text of the discussion paper "Towards Koinonia in Faith, Life and Witness",
nr.82-87). See also Th.F. Best/G. Gassmann (eds.), *On the Way to Fuller
Koinonia*, 287-289.
[9] Cf. for example, P. Tillich, *Systematic Theology*, Vol.III, Chicago 1963, 400-
407 ("The Kingdom of God and the Churches").
[10] G. Limouris (ed.), *Church Kingdom World*, 167/168 and *Fifth World Conference on Faith and Order*, 33. See also Th.F. Best/G. Gassmann (eds.), *On the way
to Fuller Koinonia*, 255.

out him who establishes it and points it in the right direction. It stresses the fact that the Church is sent: a sign exists for others; in itself it is worthless:

> *"Called by God out of the world the church is placed in the world's service; it is destined to be God's sign for the world by proclaiming the gospel and living a life of loving service to humanity. It is thus God's pointer to what God wants to tell the world and to give it. Thus the church is called constantly to look both to its Lord, to whom it owes all, and to humanity, to which it is fully committed"* [11].

If the adjective 'prophetic' is attached to the term 'sign', it is in order to recall the dimensions of judgement and salvation, and the eschatological perspective which inheres the notion of mystery, the 'open secret' of God's saving purpose to unite all things and people in Christ. The central meaning of the wide and diverse use of 'sign' in the Bible leads us to think of something pointing beyond itself and, at the same time, participating in that to which it points [12].

Above all, the concept of sign draws our attention to the way in which the unity of the Church could be of real and practical

---

[11] *Church and World*, 28. See for the church as sign also the working document "Unity of the Church – Unity of Mankind" of the Faith and Order Working Committee (Zagorsk,1973) in G. Gassmann (ed.), *Documentary History*, 137-143, esp.138.

[12] Cf. *Church and World*, 29/30. See for the meaning of the term 'sign' also the clarifications on the Lima text in, *Baptism, Eucharist & Ministry 1982-1990*, 110: "'Sign' does not simply point towards, but actually participates in, the reality which it effectively conveys. Therefore, the term 'sign' should be understood in the emphatic sense of 'effective' sign". See further *Ibid.*, 145/146: "The historical controversies on this point [i.e. on the interpretation of sacrament as sign] have arisen on the basis of different philosophical interpretations of 'sign' (*signum*) in East and West and between the churches of the West themselves concerning the relation between the signified reality (*res*) and the mediating sign (*signum*). More research could be done on the relation of the sacraments to the biblical notion of 'semeion', the idea of the sign of the covenant and the narrative structure of the prophetic sign-actions of the prophets of Israel and in the ministry of Jesus". Cf. R. Hotz, *Sakramente im Wechselspiel zwischen Ost und West*, Köln-Gütersloh 1979, 32, 38, 41, 50/51 and 60; M.E. Brinkman, *Schepping en Sacrament*, 89-99 and Groupe des Dombes, *L'Esprit Saint, l'Église et les Sacrements*, Taizé 1979, 22-25.

importance for humankind. Taking the sign-character of the Church seriously will lead us to ask where the Church's practice takes on the character of a sign. Where does the sign become visible in an exemplary way?[13] The calling to be a sign urges the churches to modesty and self-criticism on the one hand, and courage on the other hand. The Church is no more than a sign, which points beyond itself, in its proclamation of the Kingdom of God. Whenever the churches fail to reflect the community of love, justice, freedom and peace, they fail to be the sign of the Kingdom which is their vocation. Whenever they acknowledge failures and repent of them, they stand as a sign of the divine grace and hope for a broken world. To be an authentic prophetic sign, the historical and cultural dimension of the Church and its pastoral work must be constantly renewed by the Spirit. Despite human sinfulness, the love of God in Christ is mediated to God's people in such a way that, being judged and justified, they are set free to receive grace that makes them acceptable before God and initiates the process of sanctification of the world[14].

[13] Cf. G. Müller-Fahrenholz, *Unity in Today's World*, 75.
[14] *Fifth World Conference on Faith and Order*, 36 (text of the discussion paper "Towards Koinonia in Faith, Life and Witness", nr. 85). See also Th.F. Best/G. Gassmann (eds.), 288.

CHAPTER VIII

ECUMENICALS AND EVANGELICALS

Introduction

This chapter begins with a critical exposition of the possibility of giving strictly distinct descriptions of Ecumenicals and Evangelicals. Next, on the basis of a periodization of the relation between Ecumenicals and Evangelicals, from confrontation to mutual recognition, a brief outline will be given of the present situation after the Seventh World Assembly of the World Council of Churches at Canberra in 1991. That situation is considered to be characterized by a shifting of the front, in which Ecumenicals and Evangelicals are now facing the new common challenge posed to Christians of both the southern and the northern hemisphere by the radical inculturation of the gospel.

We concentrate on the developments between the more or less institutional Ecumenical and Evangelical Movement. At first sight, the description of these developments seems to be exclusively an internal Protestant discussion. Nothing could be further from the truth, however. The Roman Catholic Church is – as already stated in chapter I – full member of the Commission on Faith and Order and therefore an official participant in the institutional Ecumenical Movement. At the same time, this church has, as a kind of undercurrent, a strong charismatic movement with many contacts with the broader Evangelical Movement. In a certain sense, this church belongs to the Evangelical Movement as well. Therefore, the next description will be more an inclusive Christian one than an exclusive Protestant one[1].

---

[1] See B. Meeking/J. Stott (eds.), *The Evangelical-Roman Catholic Dialogue on Mission 1977-1984: A Report*, Grand Rapids 1986. The issues dealt with in this

The Inadequacy of Distinct Descriptions

Of course it is quite simple to define Ecumenicals as Christians strongly focussed on institutional church unity and often possessed of a deep social concern and to define Evangelicals as Christians strongly focussed on personal conversion and the spiritual unity of all Christians with a less outspoken social concern.

However, it is both ecumenically and methodically hazardous to beginn the discussion between different currents in Christianity with an isolated description of a separate current. As early as 1952, at the Third World Conference of Faith and Order at Lund, the following 'confession' was agreed upon: "We have seen clearly that we can make no real advance towards unity if we only compare our several conceptions of the nature of the Church and the traditions in which they are embodied. But once again it has been proved true that as we seek to draw closer to Christ we come closer to one another. We need, therefore, to penetrate behind our divisions to a deeper and richer understanding of the mystery of the God-given union of Christ with His Church. We need increasingly to realise that the separate histories of our Churches find their full meaning only if seen in the perspective of God's dealing with His *whole* people"[2].

In his evaluation of more than 25 years of theological reflection within Faith and Order, Lukas Vischer has the following comment on this passage: "This statement is of far-reaching importance. For it alters, so to speak, the perspective. Whereas up till then the

volume show that the claim of the inclusive character of the Ecumenical-Evangelical dialogue can be justified. Cf. further from the Roman Catholic side, P. Hocken, "Ecumenical Dialogue: The Importance of Dialogue with Evangelicals and Pentecostals", *One in Christ* 25 (1994) 101-123 and the text of the North American Evangelical-Roman Catholic dialogue published under the title, "Evangelicals and Catholics: The Christian Mission in the Third Milennium", *Catholic International* 5 (1994) 384-394. See also P.G. Schrotenboer, *Roman Catholicism: A Contemporary Evangelical Perspective*, Grand Rapids (1987) 1992[3.]

[2] *The Report of the Third World Conference at Lund, Sweden August 15-28* (Faith and Order Paper No. 15), London 1952, 5. Also quoted in chapter I ("Short History of Faith and Order).

churches had stood confronting one another, now a common point of view had been achieved which gave the necessary direction to their conversation .... They no longer ask primarily what are the features which distinguish them from other churches, but seek rather to see the differences which separate them in the light of the common relationship to the living Lord of the Church ..."[3].

In his survey of the history of Faith and Order, in the *Dictionary of the Ecumenical Movement*, Lukas Vischer's successor as director of Faith and Order, Günther Gassmann, therefore states that Lund "moved from the comparative method to a form of theological dialogue which approaches controversial issues from a common biblical and Christological basis"[4].

In view of the variety of historical dynamics and the regional variety of the different traditions, it is a highly dubious undertaking, from both an ecumenical and a more neutral methodical point of view, to employ a separate, isolated description of the various currents and orientations in Christianity. That is the reason for the crisis which so-called comparative ecclesiology has been undergoing for quite some time. Starting from the idea that every vital movement is characterized by a great measure of diversity and historical dynamics, it is well-nigh impossible to develop a sound methodology for such a comparison. To a greater or lesser degree, the aforementioned regional diversity and varying historical dynamics apply to all Christian denominations. In general the following rule can be applied: the greater the influence of congregationalism, the greater the diversity[5].

Apart from these ecumenical and methodical objections, there is also a more fundamental theological comment to be made with respect to an isolated description of ecclesiastical positions. Not

[3] L. Vischer (ed.), *A Documentary History*, 14.
[4] *Dictionary of the Ecumenical Movement*, 411-412.
[5] See on Congregationalism as a Christian denomination, W. Walker, *The Creeds and Platforms of Congregationalism*, Philadelphia/Boston (1893) 1969[2]; N. Goodall (Hrsg.), *Der Kongregationalismus* (Die Kirchen der Welt, Bd. XI), Stuttgart 1973 and M. Nijkamp, *De kerk op orde. Congregationalisme. De derde weg in de kerk van de toekomst*, 's-Gravenhage 1991.

only does such a description suggest an isolation which, in fact, hardly ever occurs, it also suggests an autonomy and independence of theological positions which cannot be justified for inherently theological reasons. Each movement in Christianity is known to carry with it, as an undercurrent or as a continuous challenge or impulse from within, the movements which it officially opposes from outside.

Not only is it impossible to describe a movement without pointing out the undercurrents within the main current, but it is also impossible to arrive at a proper understanding of a movement without taking into account the interaction with other movements. Lutheranism and Calvinism are already hardly conceivable without each other, let alone without Roman-Catholicism. And this also applies to quite a lot of cross-layers within Christianity. Low Church people are inconceivable without High Church people and Ecumenicals are likewise – and that is precisely the point I would like to make in these preliminary reflections – inconceivable without Evangelicals.

In view of these considerations, I prefer to describe the phenomenon of 'Ecumenical' in a way which from the very beginning takes into account the interaction with the phenomenon of 'Evangelical'. The price which has to be paid for such a way of approach is that of the impossibility of a presupposed, clear-cut definition. The fundamental recognition, however, of the inadequacy of describing Ecumenicals without the interaction with Evangelicals seems to me so important that I am inclined to pay that price and settle for only a very formal description of the word Ecumenical and the word Evangelical as a starting-point for the description of a dynamic process. Such a formal description might take the form of a reference to the official forms of cooperation within organizations, such as the World Council of Churches and the many regional and national Councils of Churches, as a characterization of the ecumenical position on the one side, and the World Evangelical Fellowship and the Lausanne Committee for World Evangelization as a characterization of the evangelical position on the other side. One might speak of an ecumenical or evangelical attitude, wherever, in one way or another, people feel a certain involvement in these forms of cooperation[6].

Assemblies as Landmarks

As a central point for a contemporary description of the discussion between Ecumenicals and Evangelicals, I will point specifically to the developments during and after the Seventh Assembly of the World Council of Churches at Canberra (1991). In the literature about the Ecumenical Movement it is often common practice to point to great world-wide assemblies as landmarks for important changes. I will follow that usage, although I realize that this line of approach cannot (any longer) be taken for granted and therefore needs to be justified to some extent.

The concentration on the impact of world-wide assemblies finds expression in a strong fixation on the organized 'official' ecumene between institutional churches. Apart from that, it will be a good thing for us to realize that there is also a quite different and more spontaneous kind of ecumene, such as, for example, that of the church hymn which is sung all over the world, that of prayer which transcends borders between churches and countries – finding expression, among other things, in the World Day of Prayer, which already dates from 1927 – that of the witness of the Christian martyrs from the present and the past and that of common religious service in situations of emergency. Without wishing to min-

---

[6] For very short introductions see the articles on "Evangelicals", "Lausanne Committee for World Evangelization, "World Evangelical Fellowship" and "World Council of Churches" in the *Dictionary of the Ecumenical Movement*, 393-395; 594-595; 1100-1101 and 1083-1100. See further especially D.M. Howard, *The Dream That Would Not Die: The Birth and Growth of the World Evangelical Fellowship 1846-1986*, Exeter 1986; M. Ellingsen, *The Evangelical Movement: Growth, Impact, Controversy, Dialogue*, Minneapolis 1988; R.C. Bassham, *Mission Theology: 1948-1975: Years of Worldwide Creative Tension Ecumenical, Evangelical and Roman Catholic*, Passadena 1979; M. Kinnamon, *Truth and Community*, 99-107 and T.M. Smith, "A Historical Perspective on Evangelicalism and Ecumenism", *Mid-Stream* 22 (1983) 308-325.

imize the importance of these forms of spontaneous ecumene – quite the contrary, I am rather inclined to call this ecumene the most important and the one which holds the richest perspectives – the position may very well be defended that, for a representative assessment of the situation within institutional Christianity, world assemblies are still a good indication. In view of the caution with which, increasingly, the representativeness of the composition of the delegations is assured, I am by no means inclined to neglect the warning function of these meetings. Voice and opposing voice are frequently heard here, sometimes even so frequently that it is not always easy to recognize dominant voices and important opposing voices.

Therefore, assemblies are still suitable landmarks for tracing certain developments which occasionally have great consequences for the situation of Christianity in the world. Certainly, in retrospect, the point may be made that, fairly often, tendencies have manifested themselves which afterwards actually also proved to be permanent developments. This indeed justifies my boldness in formulating certain expectations on the occasion of the last World Assembly of the World Council of Churches at Canberra. However, before giving an analysis of this assembly, it seems prudent to place the encounter Ecumenicals-Evangelicals against the historical background of a number of previous assemblies. In a sense, three periods may then be distinguished. In the first place, there is a period of a widening gap between Ecumenicals and Evangelicals, followed by a period of mutual recognition and appreciation and, finally, a period of radical changes of the front, in which Ecumenicals and Evangelicals are now partly standing shoulder to shoulder, facing new developments which are occurring particularly in the churches of the southern hemisphere, but with great consequences for the northern churches as well[7].

---

[7] In 1988 the South African missiologist David Bosch distinguished two periods: one of confrontation (1966-1973) and one of convergence (1974-1988). Not only do we ourselves take a broader view of the periodization, but after Canberra we also add a third period of common challenge. See D.J. Bosch, "'Ecumenicals' and 'Evangelicals': A Growing Relationship?", *The Ecumenical Review* 40 (1988), 458-472.

A Period of Confrontation

The period which is marked by the Third World Assembly of the World Council of Churches at New Delhi (1961), the Fourth at Uppsala (1968), the Fifth at Nairobi (1975), and which was more or less closed at the Sixth World Assembly at Vancouver (1983), was characterized by a growing contrast between what was sometimes called 'World Council of Churches theology' in a derogatory sense, and the international Evangelical Movement, which manifested itself more and more emphatically as an alternative World Council of Churches[8]. The 1960's was the period in which the Ecumenical Movement and many churches related to it celebrated the idea of secularization, interpreted in a positive sense as involvement in the world, as the world providing the church with its agenda[9].

Bonhoeffer's 'religionless Christianity' and the strong emphasis on 'socio-political involvement' appeared to be replacing many classical approaches[10]. Or, to use the words of Margaret Nash in her study on the Ecumenical Movement in the sixties, notably after Uppsala (1968): "Whereas the theological tenor of previous assemblies had been Barthian, with major emphasis on the revelatory in-breaking activity of God in Christ, Uppsala showed the growing influence of Bonhoeffer ..."[11].

[8] Cf. M. Ellingsen, *The Evangelical Movement*, 285-294 ("The Ecumenical Movement and the Proclamation of the Gospel in Contemporary Society"), esp. 287: "It is particularly in the organized ecumenical movement, Evangelicals believe, that one can identify the shotgun marriage of theology and humanism manifesting itself in a kind of theological pluralism which denies normative beliefs .... 'Ecumenism' functions as an Evangelical code word to describe all that is wrong with the contemporary church. The ecumenical movement, and particularly the World Council of Churches, is accused of having compromised biblical authority and adopted a 'socio-political understanding of the gospel'".
[9] See for a short survey of the use of the term secularization in the West, R. van der Zwan, "Searching for Indian Secularization", *Exchange* 19 (1990) 91-151, esp. 93-104. See further A. Houtepen, *Theology of the 'Saeculum': A Study of the Concept of 'Saeculum' in the Documents of Vatican II and of the World Council of Churches 1961-1972*, Kampen 1974. Cf. for an extremely positive interpretation A.Th. van Leeuwen, *Christianity in Worldhistory: The Meeting of the Faiths in East and West*, Edinburgh 1964.
[10] D.J.Bosch, "Ecumenicals' and Evangelicals'", 462.
[11] M. Nash, *Ecumenical Movement in the 1960s*, Johannesburg 1975, 320.

Whether Bonhoeffer's influence on theological thinking in the
World Council has indeed been so great is probably still open to
discussion[12]. In any case, there has been an undeniable change of
accent towards a more 'horizontal' interpretation of Christian mes-
sianism. "Many Christians are now discerning the activity of the
Spirit in the emergence of free nations, in international groupings,
and in projects where Christians and non-Christians seek together
for peace and justice in the new social structures created by the
technological revolution overtaking all societies", according to
Meredith Handspicker in a survey of the developments within
Faith and Order during the years 1948-1968[13].

It was not so much the continuous attention to the unity of the
church – which, among other things, found expression in a remarkable report on the relation of Scripture and Tradition at the Fourth
World Conference of Faith and Order at Montreal in 1963 and cul-
minated in the Lima text on baptism, eucharist and ministry – but
especially the anti-racism fund, known as the Program to Combat
Racism (PCR), established by the World Council, that roused vehe-

[12] Cf. Berkhof's short analysis of the background of the 'WCC theology': "The
origin and the history of the World Council of Churches have been shaped by many
forces but by none so deeply as by Anglo-Saxon Protestantism, with its amalgam
of Calvinist theocracy, British pragmatism and the optimistic American belief in
progress. European theology has certainly exercised its influence but more as a cor-
rective than as an inspiration. And German Lutheran theology has undoubtedly
been the one to feel its critical remoteness most deeply. It senses here that 'fanati-
cism' which for Lutherans is the greatest of errors because it confuses the Word
and the Spirit, the Kingdom of God and the kingdom of this world, emphasizes
sanctification at the expense of justification and regards the future more as a human
task than as a gift of God. From Stockholm to Uppsala and since, European theology and especially that of German Lutheranism has raised here a warning finger,
without, however, being able to offer any alternative to the existing plan". See H.
Berkhof, "Berlin versus Geneva: Our Relationship with the 'Evangelicals'", *The
Ecumenical Review* 28 (1976) 80-86, esp. 84. See further R. Frieling, *Die Bewegung für Glauben und Kirchenverfassung 1910-1937 unter besonderer Berücksich-
tigung des Beitrages der deutschen evangelischen Theologie und der evangelichen
Kirchen in Deutschland*, Göttingen 1970, esp. 205-228 and especially on the
Barthian and Bultmannian influence in Faith and Order, C. Simonson, *The Christology of the Faith and Order Movement*, Leiden-Köln 1972, 100-120.
[13] M.B. Handspicker, "Faith and Order 1948-1968" in: H.E. Fey (ed.), *The Ecumenical Advance: A History of the Ecumenical Movement*, Vol. 2: 1948-1968,
London 1970, 170 (145-170).

ment emotions among its political and theological opponents[14]. Points of fierce criticism included especially the alleged direct support of revolutionary violence with the aid of financial means provided by this fund, and the selective character of the criticism directed against repressive regimes by the World Council. It was especially the World Council's incapacity to bring up for discussion the situation in Eastern Europe, culminating in the refusal, during the Assembly at Vancouver[15], to condemn the Russian invasion of Afghanistan that, in the eyes of many people – and by no means only of the Evangelicals[16] – seriously injured the credibility and integrity of the World Council of Churches. In retrospect it seems indeed justified to blame the World Council for serious failure as regards its policy with respect to Eastern Europe. Even the most extreme accusations of communist infiltration into the Central Committee of the World Council, through KGB contacts of Russian church leaders, prove to have been right in retrospect[17].

[14] Cf. M. Ellingsen, *The Evangelical Movement*, 288: "In any case, much of the real 'heat' of controversy between Evangelicals and ecumenism emerges over the sensitive question of the WCC's political involvements, notably its Program to Combat Racism".

[15] Cf. D. Gill (ed.), *Gathered for Life: Official Report VI Assembly World Council of Churches, Vancouver, Canada, 24 July-10 August 1983*, Geneva-Grand Rapids 1983, 161/162 ("Resolution on Afghanistan").

[16] See for example the strong critique of the then director of the Interuniversary Institute for Missiological and Ecumenical Research in Utrecht (The Netherlands), H. Hebly, *Eastbound Ecumenism: A Collection of Essays on the World Council of Churches and Eastern Europe*, Amsterdam 1986, esp. chapter IV: "The Constraints of the World Council of Churches in Relationship with Churches from the Soviet Union", 59-110 and chapter V: "The World Council of Churches and Religious Liberty", 111-137. See further the remarks of H. Berkhof during the discussion on the violence—non-violence issue in the Central Committee in 1973: "Dr. H. Berkhof, Netherlands Reformed Church, regretted the necessity of omitting the reference to the Eastern European situation, but felt that this must simply be recognized as a 'taboo' issue – like that of the universal council." Cf. *The Minutes and Reports of the Twenty-Sixth Meeting of the Central Committee of the World Council of Churches*, Geneva 1973, 21. In any case, during the ensuing discussion an amendment was adopted which contained very carefully worded criticism of the restriction of religious liberty in Eastern Europe (*op. cit.*, 22).

[17] See W. van den Bercken, *Christian Thinking and the End of Communism in Russia*, Zoetermeer 1993, 133: "Another problem which has arisen for the Russian Orthodox Church as a result of the demise of the Soviet state is the opening up

The fact that, at the World Conference of Church and Society at Geneva in 1966, the World Council of Churches publicly discussed the legitimacy of socio-political revolutions came as a tremendous shock to many people in the West, even though, more than 25 years later, the formulations chosen in the Message of the conference strike one as highly balanced. It is pointed out that in the past, we, as Christians, took part in all kinds of changes in society through quiet efforts at social renewal, working in and through the established institutions according to their rules. And the text goes on to state that today a significant number of those who are dedicated to the service of Christ and their neighbour assume a more radical or revolutionary position. Discussing the theme of violence and non-violence, the conference continued the ecumenical tradition of endorsing both pacifist and 'just war' principles. On the one hand, the clear Christian teaching regarding the respect for persons and love of one's enemy requires the respect for all possible peaceful and responsible non-violent means of action in society. On the other hand, the question must be faced whether the violence which sheds blood in planned revolutions may not be a lesser evil than the violence which, though bloodless, condemns whole populations to perennial despair[18].

---

of the KGB-archives. As a result of disclosures of a Russian parliamentary committee in January 1992, the position of three prominent church leaders has been seriously undermined. In the reports of the Fourth Department (for church affairs) of the Fifth Directorate of the KGB the examining committee found out that since 1967 three metropolitans worked as informers for the KGB in ecumenical organizations, at peace conferences, at receptions of foreign delegations and in the persecutions of church disssidents. The agents indicated in the documents as Antonov, Adamant and Abbat have been identified as the respective metropolitans Filaret of Kiev, Yuvenali of Krutitsi and Pitirim, the Head of the publicity department of the Russian Orthodox Church for many, many years".

[18] See *World Conference on Church and Society: Christians in the Technical and Social Revolutions of our Time, Official Report*, Geneva 1967, 49 and 115. See further R. Jeurissen, "Peace in the Ecumenical Movement", *Exchange* 16 (1987), 1-118, esp. 25; E. Adler, *A Small Beginning: An Assessment of the First Five Years of the Program to Combat Racism*, Geneva 1974, 32/33 and *Racism in Theology and Theology against Racism: Report of a Consultation Organized by the Commission Faith and Order and the Programme to Combat Racism*, Geneva 1975, 13.

Although it is always difficult to assess exactly whether and, if so, how political and theological motives interact, it is at any rate evident that surely since 1965, more attention has been paid, within the World Council of Churches, to communal social problems than to individual existential questions of religion. According to Berkhof, the chief cause of this shift has not lain in the World Council of Churches itself but in the rapid growth of tension between the First and Third Worlds. The Council has taken this to be a central challenge to which it has responded by increasing its statements and activities in the field of social and political ethics. New concepts like 'development', 'revolution', 'racism', 'liberation' advance to the centre of the stage[19].

Berkhof recognizes that next to the positive side, namely, the right response to the 'command of the hour', there is a negative side to this development as well, namely, the danger of the 'ideologizing' of the Christian message. We need – so he stresses – to make a distinction here. An ideology is not in itself a bad thing. It is in fact the choice of perspectives, goals and rules which enable us to tackle a situation actively. An ideology in the sense of a conscious choice of principles from the Gospel is simply essential for programmes of a social and ethical kind. However, there is always the danger that such a choice is no longer regarded as a temporary selection from the richness of God's Word, a selection which must constantly be understood in terms of the Word of God, and inspired, criticized and put in its proper perspective by the richness of that Word. Where this does not find place ideology becomes an idol. It is in this context that Berkhof overtly acknowledges that "many evangelical terms such as justice, renewal, reconciliation, fellowship, liberation, etc. have acquired an ideological function in the World Council of Churches. With a view to their social and ethical utility they take on a much more restricted meaning than is proper to them in biblical usage: 'righteousness' then becomes not so much the righteousness which is given as the righteousness which is demanded; 'liberation' not so much deliverance from our

---

[19] H. Berkhof, "Berlin versus Geneva", 83.

own sins but rather from the social and political sins of others, and so on"[20].

To some people, this trend appears to be no more than a later edition of the social gospel of an earlier day[21] and a programme for an exclusively activist church; for others, however, this involvement is bound up with a truer recovery of the meaning of the prophetic tradition, the implications of the incarnation and the consequences of God's redeeming work for the person-in-society no less than for the person in his or her solitariness. Yet – so Norman Goodall states – "at the heart of the unresolved tensions at Uppsala ... there was a widely shared determination to resist any either/or resolution of the dilemma. What was being sought, ... is a deeper apprehension of what is implied by the 'point of intersection' between the vertical and the horizontal. At this point no aspect of human need is irrelevant to the Gospel .... But it does so at a point where the sin of man involves the intersecting Cross and where the mystery of death, violent and premature, exposed the most awful dimension of human existence. Because of the nature of that intersecting Cross and all for which it stands, the Church has a word to say to human need in its totality and to the world in all its spendours and failures, which is uniquely the saving Word"[22].

Immediately after Uppsala, therefore, in the Uppsala report, Visser 't Hooft argued strongly in favour of keeping together the 'horizontal' and 'vertical' line within the World Council on the principle of "No horizontal advance without vertical orientation". "We believe", he wrote in 1968, "that, with regard to the great tension between the vertical interpretation of the Gospel as essentially concerned with God's saving action in the life of individuals, and the horizontal interpretation of it as mainly concerned with human relationships in the world, we must get out of that rather

---

[20] H. Berkhof, "Berlin versus Geneva", 84.
[21] Cf. W.A. Visser 't Hooft, *The Background of the Social Gospel in America*, Haarlem 1928.
[22] N. Goodall, *Ecumenical Progress: A Decade of Change in the Ecumenical Movement 1961-71*, London 1972, 132/133.

primitive oscillating movement of going from one extreme to the other, which is not worthy of a movement which by its nature seeks to embrace the truth of the Gospel in its fullness. A Christianity which has lost its vertical dimension has lost its salt and is not only insipid in itself, but useless for the world. On the other hand, a Christianity which would use the vertical preoccupation as a means to escape from its responsibility for and in the common life of man is a denial of the incarnation, of God's love for the world manifested in Christ. The whole secret of the Christian faith is that it is man-centred because it is God-centred. We cannot speak of Christ as the man for others without speaking of him as the man who came from God and who lived for God"[23].

A Period of Convergence

In the same spirit, Bishop Arias of the Methodist Church of Bolivia addressed the Fifth World Assembly at Nairobi (1975). He proposed a 'holistic' approach – the whole gospel for the whole person for the whole world – rejecting a reduction of evangelism to 'saving souls' and of the gospel to a programme of service or social action. Social justice, personal salvation, cultural affirmation and church growth are all integral parts of God's saving acts. There are times and places where we must hold our tongues and let our witness speak through our presence and action, but such an extreme situation must not be considered normal or normative. There comes a moment when we must name the Name and proclaim the Word.

In his response to Bishop Arias' presentation, the evangelical, John Stott, while in agreement with much that Arias had said, argued that the World Council of Churches needed to recover the recognition of the lostness of humanity, the confidence in the truth of the gospel, the conviction about the uniqueness of Jesus Christ,

---

[23] W.A. Visser 't Hooft, "The Mandate of the Ecumenical Movement" in: N. Goodall (ed.), *The Uppsala Report 1968*, 313-323, esp. 317/318.

the sense of urgency about evangelism and the personal experience of Jesus Christ. Stott perceives a wide gap between Ecumenicals and Evangelicals, but he does not consider this gap to be unbridgeable: "Ecumenical leaders genuinely question whether Evangelicals have a heartfelt commitment to social action. We Evangelicals say that we have, but I personally recognize that we have got to supply more evidence that we have. On the other hand, Evangelicals question whether the World Council of Churches has a heartfelt commitment to world-wide evangelism. They say they have, but I beg this Assembly to supply more evidence that this is so"[24].

In the years after Nairobi, the adoption, by the Central Committee, of the document *Mission and Evangelism – An Ecumenical Affirmation* in 1982, can be considered as a milestone in the development of a convergence between Ecumenicals and Evangelicals[25]. This entire document is permeated by a spirit of wholeness, of refusing to tolerate any dichotomy between the 'vertical' and the 'horizontal'. In spite of the fact that a growth in common theological convictions has taken place, the report *Nairobi to Vancouver* states that two basic reciprocal challenges remain and need to be faced: "The Evangelicals ask of the World Council of Churches: How does the ecumenical movement assume and carry seriously its evangelistic responsibility vis-à-vis the billions of people who have not been reached by the gospel of Jesus Christ? Is the passion on the part of the World Council of Churches for justice to the poor matched by a similar passion for the transmis-

---

[24] See for the abstracts of Arias' presentation, "That the world may believe" and Stott's "Response to Bishop Mortimer Arias" in: D.M. Paton (ed.), *Breaking Barriers Nairobi 1975: The Official Report of the Fifth Assembly of the World Council of Churches, Nairobi, 23 November-10 December, 1975*, London-Grand Rapids, 17-19. See for the complete texts, *International Review of Mission* 65 (1976) 13-26 and 30-33.
[25] See for the complete text, *International Review of Mission* 71 (1982) 427-451 and for a study guide, J. Stromberg (ed.), *Mission and Evangelism: An Ecumenical Affirmation*, Geneva 1983. For an analysis and background information see M.R. Spindler, "Mission Reaffirmed: Recent Authoritative Statements of Churches Around the World (1982-1991)", *Exchange* 20 (1991) 161-258.

sion of the gospel to the unreached masses? In response, the World Council of Churches asks the evangelical constituency: How do we foster the unity of the church in the service of the kingdom of God? How does our missionary and evangelistic obedience embrace the total demands of the kingdom and the manifestation of the unity of the church?"[26]

In the midst of these mutual questions, recognition nevertheless appears to have been steadily growing through the years. An illustration of this is the fact that no less than three hundred Evangelicals at Vancouver signed an open letter saying that Vancouver's spiritual and biblical orientation had "challenged stereotypes some of us (Evangelicals) have had of the World Council of Churches"[27]. Although the 'open letter' still identifies two areas of disappointment – insufficient attention was given to the "invitational dimensions of evangelism" and too little was said about the spiritual alienation of individuals from God – it is strikingly positive in its assessment of the World Council of Churches. On the other hand, the influence of such an assembly should not be overrated, as appears from the report *Vancouver to Canberra*, in which it is stated that in spite of all the increasing contacts between Ecumenicals and Evangelicals and of increasing mutual recognition, the questions stated in the report *Nairobi to Vancouver* "still remain today"[28].

Partly with the help of the Methodist secretary-general of the World Council, Emilio Castro, very deliberate attempts were made during, the eighties, to bring about a deepening and therefore also an interiorization of the World Council's Christian involvement in society. It is only against that background that the theme of the Seventh Assembly of the World Council at Canberra in 1991 can be understood: Come Holy Spirit, Renew the Whole Creation!

---

[26] *Nairobi to Vancouver: 1975-1983 Report of the Central Committee to the Sixth Assembly of the World Council of Churches*, Geneva 1983, 12.
[27] D. Gill (ed.), *Gathered for Life*, 17. See for the complete text of the open letter, *Mid-Stream* 23 (1984) 127-131.
[28] *Vancouver to Canberra: 1983-1990 Report of the Central Committee to the Seventh Assembly of the World Council of Churches*, Geneva 1990, 13.

This theme is in the form of a prayer for the Holy Spirit. This prayer theme may be considered as characteristic of the ecumenical atmosphere at the end of the eighties[29]. The theme was formulated at the moment when East-West relations had reached a total deadlock and the situation in South Africa seemed hopeless. Besides, the hopes to attain a military victory followed by a rapid removal of the obstacles to an improvement of the social living conditions of the population in countries like Vietnam, Angola and Mozambique had been dashed. The feeling of human incapacity, however, also continued to exist when during the eighties, just before the Assembly, there were indeed great changes in East-West relations and in South Africa. This explains the central position of the prayer meetings during the Assembly at Canberra. After what has been stated above it comes as no surprise that the theme of Canberra was bound to meet with a great deal of approval in evangelical circles.

A Period of Common Challenge

In spite of this, the Seventh Assembly of the World Council will probably not be recorded in history as the assembly of prayer. The way in which the female Korean theologian, Chung Hyun Kyung, invoked the Holy Spirit was far too controversial for that[30]. For many Christians from the southern hemisphere, the prayers for help from the Holy Spirit appeared to act as a catalyst for a radical process of inculturation unprecedented in the eyes of many

---

[29] Cf. E. Castro, *When we pray together*, Geneva 1989. See also idem, "Evangelism, Mission, Liberation: Must we choose?" in: *Zending op Weg naar de Toekomst: Essays aangeboden aan prof.dr. J. Verkuyl*, Kampen 1978, 119-127. See further K. Raiser, "The Holy Spirit in Modern Ecumenical Thought", *The Ecumenical Review* 41 (1989) 375-386 and A. Bittlinger (ed.), *The Church is Charismatic: The World Council of Churches and the Charismatic Renewal*, Geneva 1981.

[30] See for the text of her presentation, M. Kinnamom (ed.), *Signs of the Spirit*, 37-47. Cf. also the section on "Must God remain Greek?" and on "Contextualization and Inculturalization" in chapter III.

Westerners. The theological debate at this Assembly indeed immediately concentrated on the question of the legitimacy of this call for the Spirit. There were indeed countless questions such as: how affirmatively or how critically does God's Spirit permeate our spirits, our belief?

It was precisely with regard to the legitimacy of our appeal to the Holy Spirit that an extremely fascinating shift of front occurred at Canberra. An official declaration of the Orthodox and of the Evangelicals shows that they form one united front against this form of contextualization of the Christian message. The Orthodox delegation argued that "some people tend to affirm with very great ease the presence of the Holy Spirit in many movements and developments without discernment". Against this tendency they argue: "We must guard against a tendency *to substitute a 'private' spirit, the spirit of the world or other spirits for the Holy Spirit* who proceeds from the father and rests in the Son"[31].

The Evangelicals expressed themselves in similar terms when, also in a separate statement, they said: "As the assembly discussed the process of listening to the Spirit at work in every culture, we cautioned, with others, that discernment is required to identify the Spirit as the Spirit of Jesus Christ ..."[32]. Many delegates of Baptist, Lutheran and Reformed Churches wholeheartedly endorsed the critical comments on Chung's speech and critical remarks of a similar nature could be heard from the Roman-Catholic observers[33]. Many Evangelicals and Ecumenicals were standing shoulder to shoulder, facing those who were arguing in favour of a greater measure of contextualization of the Christian message and for a more open dialogue with the other world religions. On the other hand, certainly against the background of the

---

[31] *Ibid.*, 281 (179-182).

[32] *Ibid.*, 282(282-286).

[33] See for two totally different reactions from the Roman Catholic side, T. Balasuriya, "Der Heilige Geist – ein Geist der Freiheit. Zu den beiden Einführungen ins Thema der Vollversammlung von Canberra", *Una Sancta* 46 (1991) 109-114 and A. Houtepen, "Der Heilige Geist als Quelle und Kraft des Lebens. Die pneumatologische Debatte in Canberra", *Una Sancta* 46 (1991) 92-107.

huge growth of the often evangelically-oriented independent
churches in Africa, it is clear that this is not a problem which only
concerns Evangelicals 'from outside'. Rather, it is clear that the
more strongly a community is congregationally structured and the
more it finds its adherents among the very poorest and therefore
also the illiterate, the more inevitable will be the strong interpretation of the gospel on the basis of its own situation and on the basis
of its own cultural and social background. In view of this fact, it is
conceivable that the Evangelicals, more than any other movement
in Christianity, might well be confronted with the tendency which
they so fiercely combatted at Canberra.

The gap which became manifest at Canberra between northern
Ecumenicals and Evangelicals on the one hand, and indigenous
Christians on the other hand, is not only a theological gap. It is
also an economic one. To a significant degree this is a matter of,
on the one hand, the Christians with the book and, on the other
hand, the Christians without the book, that is to say: of a contrast
between literate and illiterate, between those who can afford to
buy a book and also have had the advantage of an education, so
that they can read it, and those who have never yet been to school
and therefore have never had a book in their hands.

Walter Hollenweger, a Swiss evangelical professor of mission
with a strong ecumenical involvement, speaks here of "oral Christianity" and finds this kind of Christianity in all churches in Latin
America and Africa, but mostly in the Independent churches in
Africa and in the indigenous Pentecostal churches in the third
world. In a certain sense he reckons all these indigenous evangelical, pentecostal and charismatic Catholic and Protestant churches
among a new kind of majority(!) in Christianity – a majority forgotten up to now in the northern West and Eastern Christianity. It
is also typical of grassroot Christianity in the Roman Catholic
churches in Latin America and in many traditional mission
churches in Africa. Most of the pastors of these churches cannot
read and write.

Their spirituality is not based on books and printed liturgy or
on the personal study of the Bible, but on the experience of the

presence of God in worship and everyday life. These experiences are expressed in songs, proverbs, stories, parables and dances. The social, political and theological significance of this fast-growing[34] Christianity has so far – so Hollenweger stresses – been ignored by European Christians and theologians: "What is not printed, what exists only in songs and dances, in lives and friendship, that which is not communicated by telex and in newspapers is for them non-existent". Hence for Hollenweger the main ecumenical problem of the future is not the dialogue between Catholics and Protestants or the dialogue between free, evangelical churches and the mainline, established ecumenical churches, but much more whether or not we can inspire a viable dialogue between the oral Christians of the South and the literary Christians of the North[35].

Conclusions

On the basis of what has been stated above, I cannot but conclude that the more or less 'classical' contrast between Ecumeni-

[34] Cf. P. Hocken, "Ecumenical Dialogue", 122: "The reasons for this rapidity of growth need constant study: but they include the immediacy of experience of God, Christ and the Spirit; holistic ministry that addresses the entire person, body as well as soul, especially the ministry of healing; every-member ministry that makes all active evangelists and avoids the sclerosis of clericalism; the closeness to the people of the preachers and pastors whose limited education-formation has not alienated them from those they serve.
For these reasons, the indigenous Pentecostals have not usually absorbed the systematised rational theology of the northern Evangelicals. Their suspicion of ecumenism is generally not the ideological rejection of much conservative Evangelicalism, but the caution of the poor and barely literate in the face of the manipulation of the educated".
[35] W. Hollenweger, "The Ecumenical Significance of Oral Christianity", *The Ecumenical Review* 41 (1989) 259-265, esp. 259 and 261. See further Idem, "Towards an Intercultural History of Christianity", *International Review of Mission* 76 (1987) 526-556 and J.A.B. Jongeneel et al. (eds.), *Pentecost, Mission and Ecumenism: Essays on Intercultural Theology – Festschrift in Honour of Professor Walter J. Hollenweger*, Frankfurt-Berlin-New York-Paris-Wien 1992.

cals and Evangelicals, which manifested itself in divergent concerns for sanctification of life and a different politico-social stand,
has receded more and more into the background during the
nineties. Nowadays we may indeed speak of a cross-fertilization
between Ecumenicals and Evangelicals in many respects. In Canberra, for example, the Evangelicals formulated the common challenge for Evangelicals and Ecumenicals by using a terminology
which bears a remarkable likeness to the above-mentioned words
of Visser 't Hooft at the time of the Assembly at Uppsala: "The
challenge is to develop a theology forged in the midst of obedient
action for the sake of the gospel, so as to bring together the apostolic faith and the suffering of the oppressed, the personal and the
social, the private and the public, justification by faith and the
struggle for peace with justice, commitment to Christ and action
empowered by the Holy Spirit in the midst of the crises facing the
modern world"[36]. As in the case of the Ecumenicals in 1982, in
the paper, *Mission and Evangelism*, here, as well the supposed
opposition between personal conversion and social action has been
left far behind.

Meanwhile, a new contrast is growing, this time not between
Ecumenicals and Evangelicals, but between, roughly said, the
Christians of the northern and southern hemisphere, which in a
great many cases means: between rich and poor Christians,
between literate and illiterate, white and non-white. This contrast
is closely related to the discovery, by many non-white Christians,
that the message as it has been proclaimed to them by whites
clearly shows the features of a Western Greco-Roman process of
inculturation. Hence, the question often heard at Canberra is
raised again: "Must God remain Greek? Can Euro-American
Christian doctrines be inclusive for Afro Godtalk?"[37]. In view of
the urgency with which this question was put forward at Canberra, it is hard to avoid the impression that, after the political lib-

---

[36] *Ibid.*, 284.
[37] The book of R. E. Hood with the title *Must God Remain Greek?* was a bestseller in the assembly bookstore.

eration of the sixties and seventies which put an end to sometimes many centuries of Western political domination, a second liberation is now taking place, that is, a cultural-religious one. The emancipatory character of this process of inculturation seems indeed undeniable.

As yet, it is not clear where this process will end and on the basis of which criterion it will be judged in such a way that it is possible to distinguish clearly between syncretism and inculturation. It is, however, significant that it was those two groups within Christianity, which in the history of their development, as they themselves say, have gone farthest along the path of inculturation – the Orthodox with their liturgy in the native language and their close association with national symbols, and the Evangelicals with their bold translations of the Bible, indigenous leadership and free liturgy – which most strongly formulated the common challenge at Canberra which is contained in this process of inculturation for all Christians throughout the world.

However, they articulated only a negative challenge; they saw only the dangers. The real new challenge for Christians in the North and in the South is the biblical command to discern the spirits in the real expectation of seeing 'new things'.

The Canberra debate has brought a renewed urgency into the ecumenical exploration of gospel and culture, pointing to the need to find a new framework for the discussion in the future. "What are – to quote Wesley Ariarajah – the essential marks of a Christian and of the church in any culture? And how can Christians who can and must interpret the gospel in their own culture recognize others in other cultures as belonging to the one family in Christ? Are there real limits to diversity, or is there only a centre for the faith, and everything that comes out of and relates to that centre is a valid expression of the faith? And what are the power elements at play? For who, in the ecumenical context, has the teaching authority to say that a particular interpretation or response to the gospel in a given culture puts a person or a community outside the bounds of the church?".

In other words – so Ariarajah states – at Canberra, the gospel
and culture issue moved from being only a question of 'theologies
in dialogue' into an ecclesiological issue as well, of the church and
the churches in the context of cultural plurality[38].

---

[38] Cf. W. Ariarajah, *Gospel and Culture: An Ongoing Discussion within the
Ecumenical Movement*, Geneva 1994, 49/50.

SELECTED BIBLIOGRAPHY

History of the Ecumenical Movement

H.E. Fey (ed.), *The Ecumenical Advance: A History of the Ecumenical Movement 1948-1968*, Vol.II, London 1986² (1970).

R. Frieling, *Der Weg des ökumenischen Gedankens*, Göttingen 1992

N. Goodall, *The Ecumenical Movement: What it is and what it does*, London 1964² (1961).

M.-J. Le Guillou (ed.), *Un Nouvel Age Oecuménique*, Paris 1966.

B. Hoedemaker/A. Houtepen/Th. Witvliet, *Oecumene als leerproces: Inleiding in de Oecumenica*, Zoetermeer 1993.

N. Lossky et al. (eds.), *Dictionary of the Ecumenical Movement*, Geneva-Grand Rapids 1991.

P. Neuner, *Kleines Handbuch der Ökumene*, Düsseldorf 1984.

R. Rouse/S. Neill (eds.), *A History of the Ecumenical Movement 1517-1948*, London 1967² (1954).

J. de Santa Ana, *L'Oecuménisme et Libération*, Paris 1993.

G.H. Tavard, *Two Centuries of Ecumenism*, London 1960.

M. Van Elderen, *Introducing the World Council of Churches*, Geneva 1990.

H.J. Urban/H. Wagner (Hrsg.), *Handbuch der Ökumenik*, Bd. I, II, III/1 and III/2, Paderborn 1985-1987.

Th. Wieser (ed.), *Whither Ecumenism? A Dialogue in the Transit Lounge of the Ecumenical Movement*, Geneva 1986

Faith and Order

P. A. Crow, Jr., "The Legacy of Four World Conferences on Faith and Order", *The Ecumenical Review* 45 (1993) 13-26.

P. Crow/G. Gassmann, *Lausanne 1927 to Santiago de Compostela: The Faith and Order World Conferences, and Issues and Results of the Working Period 1963-1993* (Faith and Order Paper No.160), Geneva 1993.

H. Döring, *Kirchen – unterwegs zur Einheit: Das Ringen um die sichtbare Einheit der Kirchen in den Dokumenten der Weltkirchenkonferenzen*, München-Paderborn-Wien 1969.

K.C. Epting, *Ein Gespräch beginnt: Die Anfänge der Bewegung für Glauben und Kirchenverfassing in den Jahren 1910-1920*, Zürich 1972.

168

A. D. Falconer, "En Route to Santiago: The Work of the Faith and Order Commission from Montreal 1963 to Santiago de Compostela 1993", *The Ecumenical Review* 45 (1993) 44-54.

R. Frieling, *Die Bewegung für Glauben und Kirchenverfassung 1910-1937*, Göttingen 1970.

G. Gassmann, *Konzeptionen der Einheit in der Bewegung für Glauben und Kirchenverfassung 1910-1937*, Göttingen 1979.

G. Gassmann (ed.), *Documentary History of Faith and Order 1963-1993*, Geneva 1993.

G. Gassmann, "From Montreal 1963 to Santiago de Compostela 1993", *The Ecumenical Review* 45 (1993) 27-43.

M.B. Handspicker, "Faith and Order 1948-1968" in: H.E. Fey (ed.), *The Ecumenical Advance: A History of the Ecumenical Movement*, Vol.II, London 1970, 145-170.

Lausanne 77: Fifty Years of Faith and Order (Faith and Order Paper No. 82), Geneva 1977.

H. Meyer/L. Vischer (eds.), *Growth in Agreement: Reports and Agreed Statements of Ecumenical Conversations on a World Level* (Faith and Order Paper No. 108), New York-Geneva 1984.

J. Skoglund/J.R. Nelson, *Fifty Years of Faith and Order*, New York 1963.

T. Tatlow, "The World Conference on Faith and Order" in: R. Rouse/S.Ch.Neill (eds.), *A History of the Ecumenical Movement 1517-1948*, London 1954, 405-441.

G. Thils, *Histoire doctrinale du mouvement oecuménique*, Paris-Louvain 1962.

L. Vischer (ed.), *A Documentary History of the Faith and Order Movement 1927-1963*, St. Louis 1963.

G. Wainwright, *The Ecumenical Movement: Crisis and Opportunity for the Church*, Grand Rapids 1983.

World Council of Churches – Roman Catholic Church

A. Houtepen, "Towards Conciliar Collaboration: the WCC and the Roman Catholic Communion of Churches", *The Ecumenical Review* 40 (1988) 473-487.

J.J. Mc Donnell, *The World Council of Churches and the Catholic Church* (Toronto Studies in Theology, Vol.21), New York-Toronto 1985.

"Patterns of Relationships between the Roman Catholic Church and the World Council of Churches" (Report of the Joint Working Group), *The Ecumenical Review* 24 (1972) 247-288.

L. Vischer, "The Ecumenical Movement and the Roman Catholic Church" in: H.E. Fey (ed.), *The Ecumenical Advance: A History of the Ecumenical Movement*, Vol.II:1948-1968, London 1970, 311-352.

J. Willebrands, "Veertig jaar Wereldraad van Kerken; een katholieke reflektie", *Kosmos en Oekumene* 22 (1988) 184-191.

Ecclesiology

Th. Best/G. Gassmann (eds.), *On the Way to Fuller Koinonia: Official Report of the Fifth World Conference on Faith and Order* (Faith and Order Paper No.166), Geneva 1994.

Communio/Koinonia: A New Testament-Early Christian Concept and its Contemporary Appropriation and Significance, Strasbourg 1990.

A. Dulles, *Models of the Church: A Critical Assessment of the Church in all its Aspects*, Dublin 1976.

Fifth World Conference on Faith and Order Santiago de Compostela: Message-Section Reports-Discussion Paper (Faith and Order Paper No. 164), Geneva 1993.

A. Houtepen, "Towards an Ecumenical Vision of the Church", *One in Christ* 25 (1989) 217-237.

A. Keshishian, *Conciliar Fellowship: A Common Goal*, Geneva 1992.

J.M.R. Tillard, *Église d'églises: L'écclésiologie de communion*, Paris 1987.

G. Vandervelde, "Koinonia Ecclesiology – Ecumenical Breakthrough?", *One in Christ* 29 (1993) 126-142.

Scripture and Tradition

J. Beumer, *Die mündliche Überlieferung als Glaubensquelle* (Handbuch der Dogmengeschichte, Bd. I, Fasc. 4), Freiburg-Basel-Wien 1962.

Y.M.-J. Congar, *La Tradition et les Traditions*, Vol.I: Essai Historique, Paris 1960 and Vol.II: Essai ThÉologique, Paris 1963.

F.W. Dillistone, *Scripture and Tradition*, London 1955

Faith and Order Findings: The Final Report of the Theological Commissions to the Fourth World Conference on Faith and Order, Montreal 1963, London 1963.

A. Flannery (ed.), *Vatican II: The Conciliar and Post-Conciliar Documents*, Dublin 1975, 750-765 ("Dogmatic Constitution on Divine Revelation", 18 November 1965).

E. Flesseman-van Leer (ed.), *The Bible, its Authority and Interpretation in the Ecumenical Movement* (Faith and Order Paper No. 99), Geneva 1980.

J.R. Geiselmann, "Das Konzil von Trient über das Verhältnis der Heiligen Schrift und der nichtgeschriebenen Traditionen" in: M. Schmaus (Hrsg.), *Die mündliche Überlieferung*, München 1957, 123-206.

M. Haudel, *Die Bibel und die Einheit der Kirchen: Eine Untersuchung der Studien von 'Glauben und Kirchenverfassung'*, Göttingen 1993.

Report on Tradition and Traditions (Faith and Order Paper No. 40), Geneva 1963.

J. Reumann/J.A. Fitzmyer, "Scripture as Norm for our Common Faith", *Mid-Stream* 30 (1993) 81-107.

P.C. Rodger/L. Vischer (eds.), *The Fourth Conference on Faith and Order: The Report from Montreal 1963* (Faith and Order Paper No. 42), 50-61 ("Scripture, Tradition and Traditions").

G.H. Tavard, *Holy Writ and Holy Church: The Crisis of the Protestant Reformation*, New York-London 1959.

G.H. Tavard (ed.), *Dogmatic Constitution of Divine Revelation of Vatican Council II: Commentary and Translation*, Glen Rock 1966.

G.H. Tavard, "The Ecumenical Search for Tradition: Thirty Years after the Montreal Statement", *Journal of Ecumenical Studies* 30 (1993) 315-329.

Confessing the One Faith

G.J. Békés/H. Meyer (eds.), *Confessio Fidei: International Ecumenical Colloquium Rome, 3-8 November 1980* (Studia Anselminiana 81 – Sacramentum 7), Roma 1982.

M.E. Brinkman, "The Will to Common Confession: The Contribution of Calvinist Protestantism to the World Council of Churches Study Project *Confessing the One Faith*", *Louvain Studies* 19 (1994) 118-137.

Confessing One Faith: Towards an Ecumenical Explication of the Apostolic Faith as Expressed in the Nicene-Constantinopolitan Creed (381): A Study Document (Faith and Order Paper No. 140), Geneva 1987.

Confessing the One Faith: An Ecumenical Explication of the Apostolic Faith as it is Confessed in the Nicene-Constantinopolitan Creed (381) (Faith and Order Paper No. 153), Geneva 1991.

An Ecumenical Confession of Faith?, special issue of *Concilium*, 14 (1978) No. 8.

P. Gregorius/W.H. Lazareth/N.A. Nissiotis (eds.), *Does Chalcedon Divide or Unite? Towards Convergence in Orthodox Christology*, Geneva 1981.

S.S. Harakas, "Must God Remain Greek?", *The Ecumenical Review* 43 (1991) 194-199.

R.E. Hood, *Must God Remain Greek? Afro Cultures and God-Talk*, Minneapolis 1990.

H.G. Link (ed.), *Confessing our Faith around the World*, Vol. II (Faith and Order Paper No. 120) Geneva 1983; Vol. III: The Caribbean and Central America (Faith and Order Paper No. 123), Geneva 1984 and Vol. IV: South America (Faith and Order Paper No. 126), Geneva 1985.

H.G. Link (ed.), *The Roots of Our Common Faith: Faith in the Scriptures and in the Early Church* (Faith and Order Paper No. 119), Geneva 1984.

H.G. Link (ed.), *Apostolic Faith Today: A Handbook for Study* (Faith and Order Paper No. 124), Geneva 1985.

H.G. Link (ed.), *One God, One Lord, One Spirit: On the Explication of the Apostolic Faith Today* (Faith and Order Paper No. 139), Geneva 1988.

Ch.S. Song (ed.), *Confessing our Faith around the World*, Vol.I (Faith and Order Paper No. 104), Geneva 1981.

G. Vandervelde, "The Meaning of 'Apostolic Faith' in World Council of Churches' Documents" in: Th. Horgan (ed.), *Apostolic Faith in America*, Grand Rapids 1988, 20-25.

L. Vischer (ed.), *Spirit of God – Spirit of Christ: Ecumenical Reflections on the Filioque Controversy* (Faith and Order Paper No. 103), Geneva 1981.

Baptism, Eucharist and Ministry

Baptism, Eucharist and Ministry (Faith and Order Paper No. 111), Geneva 1982.

Baptism, Eucharist & Ministry 1982-1990: Report on the Process and Responses (Faith and Order Paper No. 149), Geneva 1990.

Th.F. Best (ed.), *Beyond Unity-in-Tension: Unity, Renewal and the Community of Women and Men* (Faith and Order Paper No.138), Geneva 1988.

M.E. Brinkman, "Creation and Sacrament", *Exchange* 19 (1990) 208-216.

M.E. Brinkman, *Schepping en Sacrament: Een oecumenische studie naar de reikwijdte van het sacrament als heilzaam symbool in een weerbarstige werkelijkheid*, Zoetermeer 1991.

Comité Mixte Catholique-Orthodoxe en France, *La Primauté Romaine dans la Communion des Églises*, Paris 1991.

Y.M.-J. Congar (ed.), *Sainte Église: Études et approches ecclésiologiques*, Paris 1963.

K.A. David, *Sacrament and Struggle: Signs and Instruments of Grace from the Downtrodden*, Geneva 1994.

A. van Eijk, "Episcope, episcopaat en de locale kerk" in: A. Houtepen, *De verscheidenheid verzoend? Actuele thema's uit het gesprek Rome-Reformatie*, Leiden-Utrecht 1989, 165-186.

Episkope and Episcopate in Ecumenical Perspective (Faith and Order Paper No. 102), Geneva 1980.

R. Feneberg, *Christliche Passafeier und Abendmahl: Eine biblisch-hermeneutische Untersuchung der neutestamentlichen Einsetzungsberichte* (Studien zum Alten und Neuen Testament, Bd. XXVII), München 1971.

P. Granfield, *The Papacy in Transition*, Dublin 1981.

M. Gosker, *Het Kerkelijk Ambt in het Limadocument: Een hermeneutische doorlichting en een kritische evaluatie van de Lima-Ambtstekst*, Utrecht-Leiden 1990.

Groupe des Dombes, *Vers une même foi eucharistique? Accord entre catholiques et protestants*, Taizé 1972.

Groupe des Dombes, *Pour une réconciliation des ministères: Éléments d'accord entre catholiques et protestants*, Taizé 1973.

Groupe des Dombes, *Le ministère épiscopal: Réflexions et propositions sur le ministère de vigilance et d'unité dans l'Église particulière*, Taizé 1976.

Groupe des Dombes, *L'Esprit Saint, l'Église et les Sacrements*, Taizé 1979.

Groupe des Dombes, *Le ministère de communion dans l'Église universelle*, Paris 1986.

A. Houtepen, "De Petrusdienst van de bisschop van Rome" in: A. Houtepen (ed.), *De verscheidenheid verzoend? Actuele thema's uit het gesprek Rome-Reformatie*, Leiden-Utrecht 1989, 111-138.

A. Houtepen/C. van Ligtenberg/B. Veldhorst, *Bibliography on Baptism, Eucharist and Ministry (Lima Text) 1982-1987*, Leiden-Utrecht 1988.

K. Kertelge (Hrsg.), *Das Kirchliche Amt im Neuen Testament* (Wege der Forschung, Bd. CDXXXIX), Darmstadt 1977.

W. Klausnitzer, *Das Papstamt im Disput zwischen Lutheranern und Katholiken: Schwerpunkte von der Reformation bis zur Gegenwart* (Innsbrucker theologische Studien, Bd. 20), Innsbruck-Wien 1987.

K. Lehmann/W. Pannenberg (eds.), *The Condemnations of the Reformation Era: Do they still divide?*, Minneapolis 1989.

J.F. Lescrauwaet, "Mutual Recognition of Baptism Between the Dutch Churches", *One in Christ* 6 (1970) 530-538.

One Lord, One Baptism (Studies in Ministry and Worship), London 1960.

C.F. Parvey (ed.), *Ordination of Women in Ecumenical Perspective: Workbook for the Church's Future* (Faith and Order Paper No. 105), Geneva 1980.

C.F. Parvey (ed.), *The Community of Women and Men in the Church: The Sheffield Report*, Geneva 1983.

G.A.M. Rouwhorst, *De viering van de eucharistie in de vroege kerk*, Utrecht 1992.

J.-M.-R. Tillard, *L'évêque de Rome*, Paris 1982.

M. Thurian (ed.), *Ecumenical Perspectives on Baptism, Eucharist and Ministry* (Faith and Order Paper No. 116), Geneva 1983.

M. Thurian/G. Wainwright (eds.), *Baptism and Eucharist: Ecumenical Convergence in Celebration* (Faith and Order Paper No. 117), Geneva 1983.

M. Thurian (ed.), *Churches respond to BEM*, Vol.I-VI (Faith and Order Paper Nos. 129; 132; 135; 137; 143 and 144), Geneva 1986-1988.

G. Vandervelde (ed.), *The Holy Spirit: Renewing and Empowering Presence*, Winfield 1989.

J.E. Vercruysse, "Sacramenten in oecumenisch perspectief" in: J. Lamberts (ed.), *Hedendaagse accenten in de sacramentologie. Verslagboek van het elfde liturgiecolloquium van het Liturgisch Instituut van de K.U.Leuven – oktober 1993*, Leuven-Amersfoort 1994, 135-155.

G. Vischer, *Apostolischer Dienst: Fünfzig Jahre Diskussion über das kirchliche Amt in Glauben und Kirchenverfassung*, Frankfurt 1982.

Church and Kingdom

Th. F. Best/W. Granberg-Michaelson (eds.), *Costly Unity: Koinonia and Justice, Peace and Creation*, Geneva 1993.

Church and World: The Unity of the Church and the Renewal of Human Community (Faith and Order Paper No. 151), Geneva 1990.

G. Limouris (ed.), *Church Kingdom World: The Church as Mystery and Prophetic Sign* (Faith and Order Paper No. 130), Geneva 1986.

G. Müller-Fahrenholz, *Unity in Today's World: The Faith and Order Studies on 'Unity of the Church – Unity of Humankind'* (Faith and Order Paper No. 88), Geneva 1978.

D.P. Niles (ed.), *Between the Flood and the Rainbow: Interpreting the Conciliar Process of Mutual Commitment (Covenant) to Justice, Peace and the Integrity of Creation*, Geneva 1992.

W.A. Visser 't Hooft, *The Background of the Social Gospel in America*, Haarlem 1929.

W. Weisse, *Praktisches Christentum und Reich Gottes: Die ökumenische Bewegung Life and Work 1919-1937*, Göttingen 1991.

Ecumenicals – Evangelicals

H. Berkhof, "Berlin versus Geneva: Our Relationship with the 'Evangelicals'", *The Ecumenical Review* 28 (1976) 80-86.

A. Bittlinger (ed.), *The Church is Charismatic: The World Council of Churches and the Charismatic Renewal*, Geneva 1981.

D.J. Bosch, "'Ecumenicals' and 'Evangelicals': A Growing Relationship?", *The Ecumenical Review* 40 (1988) 458-472.

E. Castro, "Evangelism, Mission, Liberation: Must we choose?" in: *Zending op Weg naar de Toekomst. Essays aangeboden aan prof.dr.J. Verkuyl*, Kampen 1978, 119-127.

M. Ellingsen, *The Evangelical Movement: Growth, Impact, Controversy, Dialogue*, Minneapolis 1988.

R. Fung, *Evangelistically Yours: Ecumenical Letters on Contemporary Evangelism*, Geneva 1992.

J.A.B. Jongeneel et al. (eds.), *Pentecost, Mission and Ecumenism: Essays on Intercultural Theology* (Studies in the Intercultural History of Christianity, Vol.75), Frankfurt am Main-Berlin-Bern-New York-Paris-Wien 1992.

M. Kinnamon, *Truth and Community: Diversity and Its Limits in the Ecumenical Movement*, Grand Rapids-Geneva 1988.

W. Künneth/P. Beyerhaus (Hrsg.), *Reich Gottes oder Weltgemeinschaft? Die Berliner Ökumene-Erklärung zur utopischen Vision des Weltkirchenrates*, Liebenzell 1975.

B. Meeking/J. Stott (eds.), *The Evangelical-Roman Catholic Dialogue on Mission 1977-1984: A Report*, Grand Rapids 1986.

Mission and Evangelism – An Ecumenical Affirmation, International Review of Mission 71 (82) 427-451.

K. Raiser, "The Holy Spirit in Modern Ecumenical Thought", *The Ecumenical Review* 41 (1989) 375-386

P.G. Schrotenboer, *Roman Catholicism: A Contemporary Evangelical Perspective*, Grand Rapids (1987) 1992[3].

T.L. Smith, "A Historical Perspective on Evangelicalism and Ecumenism", *Mid-Stream* 22 (1983) 308-325.

J. Stromberg (ed.), *Mission and Evangelism: An Ecumenical Affirmation*, Geneva 1983.

INDEX OF PERSONS AND SUBJECTS

Walker, W., 147
Wieser, Th., 109
Willebrands, J., 15
witness, passim
Witte, J., 19

Witvliet, Th., 11, 21, 79
Word of God, passim
Zizioulas, J.D., 19
Zwan, R., van der, 151